as the States and parts of States wherein the people thereof respectively, are this day in rebellion against the United States, the following, towit:

Arkansas, Texas, Louisiana, (except the Parishes of St. Bernard, Plaquemines, Jefferson, St. Johns, St. Charles, St. James Ascension, Assumption, Terrebonne, Lafourche, St. Mary, St. Martin, and Orleans, including the City of New Orleans) Mississippi, Alabama, Florida, Georgia, South Carolina, North Carolina, and Virginia, (except the fortyeight counties designated as West Virginia, and also the counties of Berkley, Accomac, Northampton, Elizabeth City, York, Princess Ann, and Norfolk, including the cities of Norfolk & Portsmouth; and which excepted parts are, for the present, left precisely as if this proclamation were not issued.

And by virtue of the power, and for the purpose aforesaid, I do order and declare that all persons held as slaves within said designated States, and parts of States, are, and henceforward shall be free; and that the Executive government of the United States, including the Military and naval authorities thereof, will recognize and maintain the freedom of said persons.

Abraham Lincoln in 1865. This portrait is accredited to Alexander Gardner. *Courtesy, Library of Congress, NEG. # LC-USZ62-3479*

The Emancipation Proclamation

John Hope Franklin

Harlan Davidson, Inc.
Wheeling, Illinois 60090-6000

Library of Congress Cataloging-in-Publication Data

Franklin, John Hope, 1915–
    The Emancipation proclamation / John Hope Franklin.
        p.   cm.
    Originally published: Garden City, N.Y. : Doubleday,
        1963.
    Includes bibliographical references and index.
    ISBN 0-88295-907-7
    1. United States. President (1861–1865 : Lincoln).
Emancipation Proclamation. 2. Slaves—Emancipation—
United States. I. Title.
E453.F8   1995
973.7'14—dc20   94-38153
                                                    CIP

Cover design: DePinto Graphic Design

Manufactured in the United States of America
99 98 97 96 95 1 2 3 4 5 MG

For Whit

Preface

M any documents of enduring significance drift in and out of public consciousness almost cyclically. Each time the public renews its acquaintance with the document, there is a determination, not clearly articulated however, that never again will the great work be neglected. Such a time was January 1963, the centennial of the signing of the Emancipation Proclamation by President Abraham Lincoln. There were commemorative programs in many parts of the country, reproductions of the document itself were prepared, and there were the appropriate public readings. There were also numerous receptions in honor of the event, the most notable being the one given by President and Mrs. John F. Kennedy at the White House. Meanwhile, several books, written for the occasion, analyzed, commented on, and weighed the impact of the document on the Civil War and the African-American fight for freedom.

The momentum accompanying the centennial observance of the Proclamation's signing was such that at the time it would have been reasonable to predict that such a commemoration would become at least an annual affair. Within less than a year, however, Americans had put the great document behind them. The same thing would happen to the Declaration of Independence and the United States Constitution following the observances of their bicentennials in 1976 and 1987 respectively.

However, as mentioned, these periods of relative inattention also are tenuous, for the great documents have a way of returning to the fore of Americans' thoughts. Thus, in the autumn of 1992, as various groups began to ponder the desirability of doing something to honor once again the Emancipation Proclamation, a Washington, D.C., resident, Loretta Hanes, called the National Archives to inquire if they would consider placing the Emancipation Proclamation on display to commemorate its 130th anniversary on January 1, 1993. The Archivist of the United States thought well of the idea, despite the fact that it was not possible to gauge what the level of public interest would be. But when the document was indeed placed on display in the rotunda of the National Archives building, long lines formed, and for the better part of a week many thousands came to pay their respects to and gaze upon the historic document. At the special program held in the archives in observance of the event, an enormous crowd overflowed the auditorium, spilling into other rooms to witness the proceedings on in-house television monitors. I joined the Archivist, the Honorable Eleanor Holmes Norton, the Reverend Jesse Jackson, and others to comment on the significance of the document.

On that occasion, some of those who recalled that I had written a book (which had since gone out of print) to commemorate the centennial of the signing of the Emancipation Proclamation suggested that it would be fitting to reissue the work. Perhaps, they suggested further, this would help to sustain interest in the document from year to year. Indeed, in 1994, before this work was reissued, the document was again placed on display, accompanied by a brochure, specially prepared for the series Milestone Documents in the National Archives, which contains much of the address I had delivered the previous year. The brochure was presented to all who viewed the Proclamation during the week that it was on display, and it will be distributed to viewers whenever the document is on display in the future. At present it appears that the National Archives plans to display the Emancipation Proclamation with some regularity.

I derive immense satisfaction in being associated in any way with this "Milestone Document." When the original edition of this book appeared in 1963 it was widely and well received, thus adding to my satisfaction. It was published by Doubleday and Company as well by the Edinburgh University Press. I am grateful to both of those publishers for distributing the work to many parts of the world, and in particular to Doubleday for relinquishing the publishing rights, making it possible for Harlan Davidson, Inc., to reissue the work. I am especially grateful to my editor, Andrew J. Davidson, for facilitating the republication of this work. His creativity, energy, and unfailing good humor went far in making possible its reappearance in this form and thus promoting further attention to the Emancipation Proclamation.

JOHN HOPE FRANKLIN
Durham, North Carolina
February 12, 1994

Preface to
Original Edition

A full century has elapsed since Abraham Lincoln signed the final draft of the Emancipation Proclamation. A large number of people were participants in the drama that culminated in the signing; members of the Cabinet, members of Congress, Negroes, religious and civic leaders, military leaders and common soldiers, clerks and telegraph operators. Many of them have left accounts of their experiences and observations, but few if any were in a position to tell the full story. Thus, we have from the participants who left some record of their role mere fragments. And none of them was able to see the Emancipation Proclamation in its broader context and significance. Without the vantage point provided by time, they could hardly be expected to have the objectivity and perspective that the span of one hundred years provides. But without their accounts the historian would be in no position to tell the story.

While historians have dealt with the Proclamation as a phase or an aspect of the Civil War, they have given scant attention to the evolution of the document in the mind of Lincoln, the circumstances and conditions that led to its writing, its impact on the course of the war at home and abroad, and its significance for later generations. A few have devoted considerable attention to the Proclamation. In his *The Great Proclamation* Henry Steele Commager has written a delightful, brief account for children. Benjamin Quarles covers the matter in his *Lincoln and the Negro,* but his interest properly extends far beyond the Proclamation. Charles Eberstadt has written a valuable article, "The Emancipation Proclamation," that deals largely with the texts and numerous manuscripts and printed drafts of the document.

The ramifications as well as the implications of the Emancipation Proclamation seem endless, and many of them have doubtless escaped me. But I have sought to deal here with the principal outlines of the history of the document and to indicate its general significance to contemporary as well as to later generations. As a war measure its significance is, perhaps, fairly well known. As a moral force during and after the war, its importance is, to some students of the period, elusive. As a great American document of freedom it has been greatly neglected. In these and other ways I have sought to place it in its setting and give it its proper evaluation.

I am under obligation to numerous persons for their assistance. Ann Lane and Jack Stuart have been exceedingly helpful in attending to many details. John Manigaulte has generously provided me with information that is the result of his extensive work in Italian archives and libraries. The staffs of the National Archives, the Library of Congress, the Howard University Library, the Schomburg Collection, the New York Public Library, and the Brooklyn College Libary have been generous in their assistance and cooperation. The patience and understanding of my wife remain incredibly generous. I reserve to myself, however, the full responsibility for any errors or deficiencies.

JOHN HOPE FRANKLIN
Brooklyn, New York
July 4, 1962

Contents

Time of Decision

P romptly at noon on September 22, 1862, the Cabinet was called to order by the President. Every member was present, despite the fact that the President had summoned them by special messenger only a few hours before. All were certain that Lincoln had an important announcement, but they had to wait until he cleared the air of the tension and anxiety that he sensed. And he had his own way of doing it. Artemus Ward, the humorist, had sent him a book of funny stories; and the President took this occasion to share with his heads of departments one of the funniest of all, "High-handed Outrage at Utica."

His inimitable reading of the American tall tale evoked reactions that ranged from the President's own hearty laugh to the solemn grimace by Stanton, the troubled and ever-serious Secretary of War. Some were genuinely amused, while others were merely courteous. All were doubtless preoccupied with speculations about what new statement of planning or policy their chief would now spring on them.

They did not have long to wait. Soon the reading was over, and Lincoln put aside the book. His voice took on a graver tone as he began to speak:

Gentlemen: I have, as you are aware, thought a great deal about the relation of the war to Slavery; and you all remember that, several weeks ago, I read to you an Order I had prepared on this subject, which, on account of objections made by some of you, was not issued. Ever since then, my mind has been much occupied with this subject, and I have thought all along that the time for acting on it might very probably come. I think the time has come now. I wish it were a better time. I wish that we were in a better condition. The action of the army against the rebels has not been quite what I should have best liked. . . . When the rebel army was at Frederick, I determined, as soon as it should be driven out of Maryland, to issue a Proclamation of Emancipation such as I thought most likely to be useful. I said nothing to any one; but I made the promise to myself, and to my Maker. I have got you together to hear what I have written down. I do not wish your advice about the main matter—for that I have determined for myself.[1]

No problem of the war had troubled the President more than the question of slavery and what to do about it. Of the many decisions he was called on to make none caused him more uneasiness and downright agony than the one that he announced to his Cabinet on that early autumn day in 1862. But he had made the decision, and he was determined to stand by it. It was a logical decision, the result not only of the exigencies and events of the war but also of the total experience of western man in coping with the task of eradicating the evil of human bondage. The results of the Battle of Antietam, fought on September 17, were on his side. So were the precedents.

1 The Precedents and the Pressures

F or three-quarters of a century before the outbreak of the American Civil War, emancipation was in the air on both sides of the Atlantic. In England, France, Spain, Russia, and elsewhere there was talk of emancipation. Some urged it for purely humanitarian reasons. Other supporters were motivated by political and economic considerations. The new revolutionary philosophies were making demands not only for the political independence of the colonies of Europe, but also for the complete freedom of the human body and spirit.

As the European colonies in the New World opened their drive to cast off the yoke that held them to the mother country, they sought to bring consistency to their crusade by speaking out against slavery. Everywhere the climate was conducive to a consideration of the problem of human freedom. And the United States, a participant in the discussion, could hardly have escaped the impact and influence of developments elsewhere, even if it had tried.

"Slaves cannot breathe in England," the poet William Cowper said in 1783. A recent authority has suggested that Cowper was employing the license to which a poet is entitled.[1] In 1772 Lord Mansfield, in the celebrated Somersett case, declared that slavery was too odious to exist in England without specific legislation authorizing it. Neither Cowper nor Mansfield was quite precise in their pronouncements, but, by the end of the eighteenth century, the sentiments they expressed were exerting enormous influence on the attitudes of the peoples of the western world. If slavery existed in England, its days were numbered—by private attitudes and public policy. On the Continent the sentiment was even more pronounced, where French liberals saw and denounced the obvious incongruity between the great drive to liberate the human spirit and any disposition to countenance chattel slavery.

It was only natural that the New World should provide the setting for the crusade against slavery. It was in French, Spanish, and English America where sheer numbers of slaves made the problem at once more acute and more urgent. It was in these settlements, also, that the movements for independence forced the colonists to examine the whole problem of freedom, human as well as political. In the French colony of St. Domingue, leaders such as Dessalines, Christophe, and Clervaux proclaimed the independence of their island in 1803 and, at the same time, wiped out forever the institution of slavery.

In a variety of ways one new Latin American nation after another either declared political independence and human freedom simultaneously or proceeded to arrange for the emancipation of the slaves shortly after gaining political independence. They seemed to be guided by the view set forth by Dr. José Simeon Canas of the Republic of Central America who said in 1823 that when the entire nation has been declared free, "so should the individuals who compose it."[2] Argentina began its career as an independent nation amid the chaos created by the resignation of the Spanish Junta in 1810. Although the actual declaration of independence did not come until 1816, the provisional congress of 1813 began to prepare the way by instituting a series of reforms. Prominent among them was the law providing for the freedom of all children of slaves. In 1824, with the urging of Dr. Canas and other reformers, Central America, after drawing up its new constitution, enacted a law ending slavery and granting freedom to all fugitive slaves in the republic.[3]

After two attempts Mexico was successful in emancipating its slaves. In 1814, the year following its Declaration of Independence, the Mexican congress abolished slavery. Within a year the Spanish troops had returned and reestablished the old institutions, including slavery. The reinstatement of Spanish rule was short-lived, however; and soon the Mexicans were once again independent. In 1829, when the Mexican senate, dominated by wealthy slaveholders, refused to pass an emancipation bill, President Vicente Guerrero issued a decree declaring all slaves in the republic to be forever free.

In the next few years the momentum for emancipation increased. In 1831 Bolivia emancipated its slaves. In 1842 the slaves of Uruguay were set free. Within a decade the movement for emancipation had crystallized in other countries, Colombia and Argentina setting their slaves free in 1851 and 1853 respectively. In 1854 President José Gregorio Monagas of Venezuela reminded his congress that Simon Bolivar, the father of independence, had wished the slaves to be free. Accordingly a law was passed emancipating the slaves and providing for the compensation of their owners. In Peru President Ramón Castilla and the progressive newspaper, *Comercio*, led the fight that resulted in the abolition of slavery in 1855.[4] By this time only Cuba and Brazil among the Latin American countries held on to slavery. The United States, the leader in political independence, was lagging far behind in the cause of human freedom.

Well before midcentury the British had taken steps to end slavery in their New World colonies. The pressure for emancipation increased steadily both in Britain and in the colonies during the 1820s. In England the Society for the

Mitigation and Gradual Abolition of Slavery Throughout the British Dominions was gaining wide support in its crusade against slavery. In colonies, such as Jamaica, citizens declared themselves "the zealous advocates of a change from slave to free labour with a dire regard for the rights of everyone."[5] These pressures culminated in 1833 in the enactment of a bill to abolish slavery. Slaveowners were to be compensated in an amount not exceeding £20,000,000. As a method of transition for the slaves a system of apprenticeship was established. By 1838 the system had disappeared, and blacks were allowed to enter a period of responsible freedom.

As the institution of slavery became more important to the economic development of Southern agriculture, the people of the United States watched with uncommon interest the decline of slavery in other parts of the New World. The revolution that led to the emancipation of the slaves in Haiti had a profound effect on the attitudes of people in the United States toward slavery and the slave trade. South Carolinians, fearful that the revolutionary sentiment would spread to their state, forbade the importation of slaves "from Africa, the West India Islands, or other place beyond the sea" for two years beginning in 1792. In 1800 members of Congress reacted sharply to developments in Haiti. John Rutledge of South Carolina deplored "too much of this new-fangled French philosophy of liberty and equality." When a group of free blacks in Pennsylvania asked Congress to revise the laws of Congress so as to provide for eventual emancipation, Samuel W. Dana of Connecticut said that if Congress acted favorably, it would be responsible for producing "some of the dreadful scenes of St. Domingo."[6]

There were some who thought that the slave revolt in Henrico County, Virginia, in the late summer of 1800 was the beginning of the worst. Led by Gabriel Prosser, a slave from a plantation near Richmond, the unsuccessful revolt suggested to Virginians and many others the possible influence of the changes that were occurring in the black nation in the West Indies. Refugees were coming into the United States from Haiti, and they were doubtless spreading abolitionist doctrine among the slaves. Antislavery leaders in the United States never failed to utter warnings about the disaster that was sure to overtake them unless steps were taken to abolish slavery. Thus the spread of emancipation in the New World was underscoring the uniqueness of the position of the United States, and the abolitionists were making the most of it. One of their best opportunities came with the emancipation of the slaves in the British colonies.

The achievement of emancipation in the British empire was, in part, an American achievement. The collaboration between American and British antislavery leaders was extensive. Anthony Benezet, the Philadelphia schoolteacher, had done much to inspire Britain's Granville Sharp and Thomas Clarkson with his Quaker strictures against the holding of slaves. Charles Stuart, pioneer American abolitionist, went to England in 1829 to urge immediate emancipation. When emancipation was finally achieved in 1833, the delight of American abolitionists was equaled only by the depression and frustration of the proslavery element.

To the American proslavery element that feared the consequences of emancipation, the abolitionists pointed with pride to the results in the West Indies. The *American Anti-Slavery Almanac for 1839* was happy to report that in Jamaica "Institutions undreamt of in the days of slavery have been founded for agricultural, literary and scientific purposes. . . . The vices peculiar to slavery are gradually wearing away; nightly orgies and licentious practices are fast falling into disuse; concubinage is receding before matrimony, and the long night of superstition rapidly evanishing [sic] before the sun of Christianity."[7] In the years that followed, American abolitionists continued to emphasize the salutary effect of British emancipation, and their British collaborators joined them in their efforts to extend the area of freedom.

By 1860 Russia had about 1,400,000 household serfs and 20,000,000 serfs on the land. For a generation there had been some agitation to free the serfs. A considerable group of Russian intellectuals, known today as Slavophiles, were convinced that if Russia was to take its place among the leaders of the world, it should avoid the mistakes the West had made and correct the mistakes it had already made. They called for sweeping reforms including the emancipation of the serfs. It was incompatible with their view of religion, their philosophy of life, and their view of Russia and the Russian people. Calling for the abolition of bureaucracy and serfdom, Petr Kireevskii, a leading Slavophile, said that the change to be effected "should not be the intermediate stage of bondsmen, because mediation between the landlord and the peasants is impossible, but a complete division between the landlord and the peasants. . . ."[8]

There were other factors in Russian life, however, that were even more powerful than the agitation of the Slavophiles. Capitalist industry had been growing steadily since the 1820s. The employment of serfs in factories was, almost from the beginning, carefully regulated by the government. With the wages of serfs fixed by law and with other conditions of employment under government control, factory owners sought relief even if it meant emancipation of their serfs. Finally, in 1840, they were permitted to emancipate their serfs, thereby escaping government scrutiny and regulation. Indeed, as one authority has suggested, the continuation of serfdom had become anathema to the growing strength of capitalist industry.[9]

The Russian government began to take some initiative in the matter of dealing with the problem of serfs. In 1837 Czar Nicholas I created the Office of State Domains, which established for the state peasants an autonomous communal structure. This served as a model for later emancipation. In 1856 Alexander II, even more sensitive to the problem than his predecessor, declared that serfdom could not continue forever. Feeling that it would be better that the reform be

effected "from above than from below," he asked the nobil-
ity for suggestions. When they were of little help he appointed a committee to look into the matter. There ensued
a bitter debate between the agricultural landlords and the
industrial serf owners over the terms of emancipation. By
1861 a plan had been worked out to the satisfaction of the
major groups involved.[10]

Under the terms of the Russian emancipation of the
serfs, the juridical authority of the noble over his peasants
was terminated, without compensation to the former owners. The serfs, moreover, were to retain the land they had
been using. But they did not thereby achieve complete
freedom or equality. They continued to be subject to capi-
tation taxes, as well as conscription. They did not immediately become proprietors of the land and, as members of
communes, their movements were regulated by that body.
Like emancipation in so many other places, the step taken
by Russia in 1861 was only the beginning. In 1863 emancipation was extended to serfs on the imperial land. In 1866
and 1867 most of the state peasants were granted the lands
they cultivated.[11]

Developments in Russia were followed with the greatest of interest in the United States. The antislavery leaders
heaped generous praise on Czar Alexander. One called
Russian Emancipation "perhaps the greatest single legislative act in the history of the world."[12] Later Senator
Charles Sumner praised the Czar for his "unwavering initiative" in bringing about the emancipation of the serfs, secur-
ing for them an allotment of land, carrying out court reform,
and introducing the political rights of self-government. It appeared to many Americans that Russia had suddenly emerged
into the modern world and had outdistanced the United
States in its handling of the problem of human freedom.

It is impossible to measure the extent of the influence of
these developments on the course of events in the United
States. These former English colonists had their own ideol-

ogy of emancipation to which some of them were becoming more deeply committed with every passing year. If the English had their William Cowper the colonists had their Samuel Sewall, whose *Selling of Joseph* condemned the holding of slaves at the very beginning of the eighteenth century. Two generations later, when the colonists began to agitate for independence, their more articulate leaders like James Otis affirmed the blacks' inalienable right to freedom.

The truly "vehement philippic against Negro slavery," as John Adams called it, was an early draft of the Declaration of Independence. In it Jefferson arraigned the king for waging "cruel war against human nature itself, violating its most sacred rights of life and liberty in the persons of a distant people who never offended him, captivating and carrying them into slavery in another hemisphere, or to incur miserable death in their transportation thither." This was, indeed, too vehement for the Southern delegation at the Continental Congress and, upon their insistence, it was stricken from the document before its final adoption.[13]

The silence of the final draft of the Declaration of Independence on the matter of slavery and the slave trade increased the difficulty of later Americans who sought precedents for their drive against slavery. Even if Jefferson did say that all men were created equal, it was said in the context of a slave society. And no one could erase the fact that the proposed antislavery passages of the Declaration had been ruled out altogether. Even so, the implications of the Declaration, however vague, were so powerful that the defenders of slavery found it necessary to deny the self-evident truths which it expounded and to debate the abolitionists on the question of just what the Declaration meant with regard to a free society in nineteenth-century America.

Despite the equivocation of the Declaration of Independence on the question of slavery, there was no stalemate in the emancipation movement. Soldier-slaves were emancipated as a reward for their services, and many new voices spoke out against slavery. Manumission societies sprang up all over the country, and some of them achieved notable success. Even before the surrender at Yorktown the states had begun their countdown against slavery. In 1780 Pennsylvania provided for the gradual abolition of slavery. By 1783 Massachusetts had abolished slavery by asserting that the Constitution of 1780 discountenanced the institution by saying that "all men are born free and equal." In the following year Connecticut and Rhode Island passed acts that abolished slavery gradually. Manumission acts were passed in New York in 1785 and New Jersey in 1786, although effective legislation was not achieved in those states until 1799 and 1804 respectively. More free states were provided for by the Ordinance of 1787, which excluded slavery from the Northwest Territory.

Once the Northwest Ordinance was passed and the Northern states had enacted their emancipation laws, there was no further large-scale emancipation of slaves before the Civil War. The runaway slave who escaped rendition under the fugitive slave laws emancipated himself. The slave who purchased his freedom or whose master manumitted him increased the precedents and examples of freedom. The slave who escaped via the Underground Railroad was "free at last," even if the restrictions of his adopted Northern home kept him from being completely free. Some of the slaves who revolted got their freedom, but the price they paid in suffering and death was indeed high. Numerically, these were all minor steps toward freedom; but their significance was measured in the way they kept the path to freedom open, rather than in their numbers. Others could and did follow the path; and the path itself not only refuted the argument that all blacks were or should have been slaves, but it was an open invitation to those in thralldom to follow the rugged road to freedom.

Some of these American experiences set important precedents that were to influence the thoughts and actions of the nation's leaders during the Civil War. Just what could the government in Washington do about slavery? This was the question that was asked over and over again as the institution became deeply entrenched after the War of 1812. In 1819 a Representative in Congress from New York, James Tallmadge, Jr., answered the question by insisting that Congress should prohibit the further introduction of slavery into Missouri and emancipate all children of slaves there when they reached the age of twenty-five. Many of his Northern colleagues agreed with him. Although they were unable to exclude slavery from Missouri, they served notice that they would continue to insist that the federal government had the power to control and limit slavery in the United States.

During the war with Mexico in 1846 the Northern members of Congress once more spoke out in favor of the authority of the federal government over slavery. Having dragged their feet in supporting the war, they wanted to make certain that the struggle would not be turned into an instrument to promote the spread of slavery. Slavery should be prohibited in any territory acquired during the war, said Pennsylvania's David Wilmot in a rider attached to the army appropriations bill. It cleared the House but failed in the Senate, where the powerful proslavery leaders held out against it. This set the stage for the great fight to be waged in the next decade regarding the power of Congress over slavery. The fight in Kansas settled nothing except to confirm the obvious fact that neither side would yield. The decision in the Dred Scott case denying federal authority over slavery was bitterly opposed by those who looked to Washington as the keeper of the national conscience. The precedents were not at all clear in the final decade before the Civil War.

Contributing to the confusion and misunderstanding were the abolitionists themselves whose voice became louder after 1830. Power in Washington was used against freedom and in behalf of the slaveholder, they cried. Freedom of speech and petition had been curtailed in the interest of silencing criticism of slavery. The spirit of free inquiry "is the master spirit of the age," declared Representative William Slade of Vermont. "It bows to the authority of truth and reason and Revelation; but it bows to nothing else." The denial of human freedom was leading to the denial of the rights of those who were free. Since the government seemed to be under the control of the proslavery elements, some abolitionists would not even attempt to enlist its aid in behalf of freedom. To Garrison the Constitution was an "atrocious compromise," while Samuel J. May denounced it as a "sin framed by law." They could not expect anything from a government existing under such authority, and they would ask nothing of it.

More realistic opponents of slavery came to the conclusion that the cause was not quite so hopeless, and by 1840 they had begun to seek an end to slavery within the framework of the government. Many of them lived in the states created out of the Northwest Territory. They were doubtless mindful of the effectiveness of the Ordinance of 1787 that forbade slavery there. They were also aware of the growing power of the electorate in influencing policy by the choices they made at the polls. They began to rally around political parties, organizing their own when they launched the Liberty Party in 1840, and pooling their power with others in the founding of the Republican Party more than a decade later.

By 1861 the steady drive for emancipation had all but isolated the Southern slave states; and they were by the very persistence of their peculiar institution becoming more and more unique. Elsewhere in the New World, only in Cuba and Brazil had slavery survived beyond the eighteen-fifties, and in neither of those countries was there the bitter, uncompromising defense of slavery as a "positive good," that there was in the South. The emancipation of the Russian serfs in 1861 cleared the last vestige of forced labor in Europe. The existence of slavery in the pioneer democracy of the Western World placed the United States in the company of rather backward places like Cuba and Brazil and the avowedly "uncivilized" portions of Asia and Africa. It was a rather dubious distinction of which an increasing number of Americans were not proud.

As Americans looked about them they found less company, but they found more precedents. Slaves had been emancipated by legislative decree, executive order, and royal proclamation. With so many precedents of emancipation before them and with many of them within the framework of a government sorely pressed by the slaveholding element itself, surely the American people could find the power and the justification for a policy that would put them in step with the more civilized areas of the world.

With all the fire and passion that characterized it, the debate between the abolitionists and proslavery leaders seemed almost academic until the outbreak of the Civil War. As if by magic, however, the war transformed the discussion into a bitter struggle between mortal enemies. It was not yet a precise division between those who were opposed to slavery and those who favored it, for there were many among those who supported the Union who were less than lukewarm to the antislavery cause. Even in its early stages, however, and despite the statement to the contrary by Union leaders, the war sharpened the issue of slavery. And the question of emancipation remained a burning issue from the firing on Sumter in April 1861 to the end of the war in April 1865.

President Lincoln could disclaim the power to emancipate the slaves, and he and his advisers could question the wisdom of attempting it even if the power existed. But they could not make the question of freedom go away merely by their fervent desire that it should do so. Indeed, with every passing day the question forced itself upon the Washington government with greater urgency. No official could ignore it. A leader as sensitive to its importance as Lincoln would not dare do so. From the beginning, therefore, he faced it, even when he showed great reluctance to do anything about it.

In his inaugural address President Lincoln declared that he had no purpose, "directly or indirectly, to interfere with the institution of slavery where it exists."[14] A few months after Sumter, Congress passed a resolution in which it asserted that the war was not being prosecuted with the intention of overthrowing the "established institutions" of the states. President Lincoln could continue to disclaim either the power or the desire, under the circumstances, to emancipate the slaves. Congress could deny any intention of setting free a single slave. The fact remains that the pressure to do something about slavery mounted; and long before the end of the first year of the war, no one could ignore the vast implications of the war for slavery.

The pressure of the war itself was, perhaps, the most powerful force urging some definitive consideration of the question of slavery. In the early days of the war neither Lincoln nor his Secretary of War was willing to use black troops as a part of the United States fighting forces. "This Department has no intention to call into the service of the Government any colored soldiers," the Secretary of War wrote to one black volunteer. The Unitarian clergyman, Moncure Conway, found that "the mere mention of the Negro made the President nervous." But despite the fact that the Confederacy was not arming the slaves, it was using them in a variety of ways that released white Southerners for the honorable duty of bearing arms. In other words, blacks were being used to defeat the Union. Could the Union ignore this painful and indisputable fact? What would it do about it?

As early as 1837, during the debates over the proposal to lay antislavery petitions on the table, and again in 1842 John Quincy Adams provided an answer to that question. He asserted that during a war all laws governing the institution of slavery were swept aside. It was ridiculous, he argued, to claim that under such circumstances the federal government had no power to interfere in any way with slavery. When two hostile armies oppose each other the commanders of both have the power to emancipate all the slaves under their jurisdiction, he concluded. Surely, by the reasoning of Adams, the situation in 1861 provided the Union commanders with such an opportunity and imposed on them the obligation to emancipate the slaves in the interest of victory over the Confederacy.

Simon Cameron, the Pennsylvanian who got his post as Lincoln's first Secretary of War more by political influence than by ability or dedication, soon faced the situation that Adams had conceived. Slaves were being used by Confederates to promote their cause. Some, however, were rushing toward the Union lines. What should be done with them? James Redpath, the versatile, resourceful general agent for the Haitian Bureau of Emigration, had the answer. Send them to Haiti, where they would be given a home and a farm. Cameron was not convinced that this was a satisfactory solution; but he gave the proposal his serious consideration. Finally, he decided against it. Something must be done, however; and no one realized this more than the Secretary of War as he came in for more and more attack by a variety of critics.

Cameron finally reached a decision, and he set forth his recommendations in his report to the President in December 1861. The slaves should be emancipated and armed, he declared. This was as justifiable as it was for the government to use gunpowder taken from the enemy. Cameron, not content to set this proposal before the President for his consideration, distributed his report among the postmasters of the larger cities. Lincoln was outraged by what he considered to be Cameron's unauthorized action. By telegraph he ordered that the Cameron report be recalled and revised. In the revised version of the report Cameron merely asserted that the slaves were a military resource and should not be returned to their masters. Cameron's precipitate action was one more indication to Lincoln that his Secretary of War was unfit for the post. Within a month Edwin M. Stanton was Secretary of War, and Cameron had been named the United States Minister to Russia.

Cameron's forced exile to Russia did not solve the problem of emancipation or the manner in which slaves were to be used by the Union. The pressure of the Cameron report had been anticipated in May 1861 by the daring, flamboyant Benjamin Butler, who, as the commanding general at Fort Monroe, had refused to give up three slaves and, in effect, had set them free to be employed by the Union forces there. In August 1861, Major General John C. Frémont, a Republican more radical than Lincoln dared be, proclaimed martial law in Missouri and declared as free the slaves who had been confiscated from persons resisting the authority of the United States. The President was embarrassed, to say the least, for his policy was to deal gingerly and discreetly with the border slave states. In Kentucky the legislature threatened to take drastic action. On several fronts volunteers declared that they would not fight if the Frémont order remained in effect. Lincoln, therefore, ordered Frémont to show leniency as to martial law and to modify the emancipation order so as to conform to existing law.

The military pressure for emancipation continued. In March 1862, the new commander of the Department of the South, Major General David Hunter, took the matter into his own hands. He began to issue certificates of emancipation to all slaves who had been employed by the Confederacy. In April he proclaimed that the slaves at Fort Pulaski and Cockspur Island were free. In the following month he declared slaves free throughout the Department of the South. This was too much for Lincoln. On May 19 he countermanded the Hunter proclamation, declaring "that neither General Hunter, nor any other commander, or person, has been authorized by the Government of the United States, to make proclamations declaring the slaves of any State free." Lincoln made it clear that he reserved to himself the question of whether or not slaves anywhere should be set free.[15]

For several months following the outbreak of the war, there was no Congress to take cognizance of the conflict and to offer its opinion on the conduct of the struggle. From the moment that Congress met in July 1861, it began to apply pressure on the President by expressing its views and by enacting legislation that reflected its views. Some legislation was timely, indeed welcomed by the President. Other actions were of dubious value from Lincoln's point of view. Despite his growing stature and despite his attempts to influence Congressional action, the legislative branch had a mind of its own and expressed it with increasing determination as it witnessed the President's exercise of authority. The war was being conducted ineffectively, Congress declared; and it created the Committee on the Conduct of the War. It noted with alarm the disaster at Bull Run and resolved that the only legitimate aim of the war was to maintain the supremacy of the Constitution and to preserve the Union.

Congress was determined to take steps to demonstrate its authority in the conflict in other ways. On August 6, 1861, it passed the first Confiscation Act, providing that when slaves were engaged in hostile military service, the owners' claims to the labor of such slaves were forfeited.[16] Despite the vagueness of the manner of forfeiture, Congress left no doubt that it was moving toward a policy that embraced emancipation under certain conditions. Lincoln, fully aware of the far-reaching implications of the bill, signed it with some reluctance.[17] It was pressure on him that he did not relish, and it came from a source that he could not altogether ignore.

In subsequent months Congress applied greater pressure by enacting emancipation legislation that was even more significant. Congress had not bowed to abolitionist sentiment, but it was yielding to the logic of the argument that John Quincy Adams had advanced more than twenty years earlier. Slaves were, indeed, weapons of war that must not be in the hands of the enemy. Emancipation was a weapon that could be used for psychological as well as military purposes. Many discerning members of Congress fully appreciated the importance of this weapon. Representative John A. Bingham of Ohio said, "Pass your laws liberating 4,000,000 slaves . . . and let the oppressed go free. Do you say this is fanaticism?" "Yes," answered several of his colleagues; and if the slaves were set free millions now faithful "with one heart would join the foe," warned William Henry Wadsworth of Kentucky.[18]

There was no chance that Congress would pass a universal emancipation bill, and only a small minority of the members favored that. In the spring of 1862 both houses were considering a bill to emancipate the slaves of the District of Columbia, where the authority of Congress could hardly be questioned. The bill precipitated a long debate that covered everything from the Caucasian race to freedom of conscience to cannibalism. Finally, on April 11, the bill was passed abolishing slavery in the District and, at Lincoln's insistence, appropriating $1,000,000 for compensation to masters not to exceed $300 for each slave. Also at the President's insistence, the bill provided for the removal and colonization of the freedmen.[19]

The President had wanted some border state to take the first step in emancipation, and he withheld his signature for several days. Charles Sumner, the ardent abolitionist Senator from Massachusetts, rushed to the White House and urged the President to sign. Daniel A. Payne, the black bishop of the African Methodist Episcopal Church, also called on Lincoln. He asked the President if he intended to sign the bill. When the President was equivocal in his reply, Payne told him that blacks had been praying for him and expressed the hope that he would live up to their expectations.[20] Two days later Lincoln signed the bill, saying that he had "ever desired to see the national capital freed from the institution in some satisfactory way" and expressing his gratitude that Congress had seen fit to include provisions for colonization and compensation.[21]

Troubles in the District had just begun, however. Slaveholders in Maryland were furious when their slaves flocked into the nation's capital to secure their freedom. The United States Marshal for the District of Columbia, Ward H. Lamon, was overly zealous in jailing escaped slaves as violators of the fugitive slave law of 1850. The commanding general for the District, James S. Wadsworth, in turn arrested the jailer and demanded the release of the fugitive slaves. Wadsworth was relieved of his command and transferred to the Army of the Potomac.[22] The issue remained unsettled until 1864, when the fugitive slave laws were repealed.

It seemed that Congress had merely begun; and for several months it retained the initiative in the emancipation drama. On June 19, 1862, it passed and sent to the President a bill abolishing slavery in the territories.[23] There was no provision for the compensation of the masters, but the President placed his signature to the bill. He was by this time absorbed with plans to compensate masters in the District of Columbia and in the border states.[24] Slaves in the territories were, perhaps, too few in number to make an issue out of the omission.

Congress took its boldest step toward emancipation in the Second Confiscation Act, passed on July 17, 1862. It dealt with several significant problems, the most important of which were the punishment of treason, the confiscation of property, and the emancipation of slaves. The provisions were far-reaching and drastic, and the debates were acrimonious. Confiscation, said the moderates, was nothing short of revolution. Emancipation, said the slaveholders, was an advanced stage of revolution. The President was unhappy and wrote out a veto message, in which he suggested that "the severest justice may not always be the best policy." Only a joint resolution of Congress explaining that the law was not to work forfeiture beyond the life of the accused restrained Lincoln from actually vetoing the bill.[25]

As far as emancipation was concerned, the second confiscation act provided that if anyone committed treason, his slaves were free. It further provided that the slaves of all persons supporting rebellion should be "forever free of their servitude, and not again held as slaves."[26] This provision was especially disturbing to Lincoln. "It is startling to say that Congress can free a slave within a state," he said, "and yet if it were said the ownership of the slave had first been transferred to the nation, and that Congress had then liberated him, the difficulty would at once vanish." The difficulty remained, but the President went along with Congress and signed the bill. On the same day, July 17, 1862, he signed the militia act that provided that any enemy-owned slave who rendered military service would be free, together with his mother, wife, and children.

Lincoln's reluctance to take positive action against slavery during his first year in office did not stem from his affection for the institution. As a fledgling member of the Illinois legislature in 1837 he declared that "slavery is founded both on injustice and bad policy." He had not changed his mind. In 1861, however, he was acutely aware of the fact that emancipation would precipitate a crisis in the border states and that many Union soldiers were unwilling to fight to free the slaves. He also doubted the legality of the outright emancipation of slaves, especially without compensation for the owners. He also doubted that whites and freed blacks could live together in peace, and this led him to advocate colonization. Compensation and colonization were thus to dominate the President's thinking as he moved haltingly toward a policy of emancipation.

As early as November 1861, Lincoln drafted, as a trial run, two bills for compensated emancipation in Delaware. He proposed that the federal government should finance the project by selling $700,000 worth of 6 per cent bonds and paying the bill over a period of five years. He circulated the drafts of several alternative proposals among the members of the Delaware legislature, but the bill was never introduced.[27] When he delivered his annual message to Congress in 1861 he was still optimistic about the possibility of the enactment of such a bill in Delaware and in other states. He asked Congress to consider the possibility and to prepare not only to provide compensation but colonization as well.[28]

In March 1862, the President sent to Congress a special message on the question of compensated emancipation. He urged the members to provide support for states that might desire to emancipate their slaves. To that end he asked Congress to adopt a resolution, "that the United States ought to cooperate with any state which may adopt gradual abolishment of slavery, giving to such state pecuniary aid, to be used by such state at its discretion, to compensate for the inconveniences, public and private, produced by such change of system." Lincoln argued that such a measure would be one of the most efficient means of self-preservation. In a letter to Senator James A. McDougall of California he pressed this argument, asserting that "Less than one half-day's cost of this war would pay for all the slaves in Delaware at four hundred dollars per head. . . . [and] less than eighty seven days cost of this war . . . would pay for all in Delaware, Maryland, District of Columbia, Kentucky, and Missouri." These personal appeals persuaded Congress to pass the resolution, but compensated emancipation was making no headway in the states.[29]

Lincoln continued to press the matter in Congress. In conversation with members, by letter, as well as by special appeal to the members of Congress from the border states he attempted to show that compensated emancipation would have a decided effect on the course of the war. In July 1862 he sent to Congress a bill providing that "whenever the President of the United States shall be satisfied that any State shall have lawfully abolished slavery . . . either immediately or gradually, the President . . . is to pay the State in 6% interest bearing bonds equal to the aggregate value, at X dollars per head." The bill was read and committed to the Committee of the Whole House and ordered to be printed. Congress adjourned without acting on it.

The pressures of the generals and Congress were sufficient to give President Lincoln a clear understanding of the relationship of slavery to the war, if, indeed, he lacked such an understanding. His response to these pressures indicates not only that he fully appreciated this relationship, but that he was constantly seeking a way to give meaning to it and, at the same time, promote the Union cause. The pressures of individuals and groups added to the President's woes without contributing to a practical solution of the problem.

The war had hardly begun before the uncompromising senior Senator from Massachusetts, Charles Sumner, began to urge upon the President the outright emancipation of the slaves. As a leading Republican he had regular access to the White House and he did not fail to take advantage of his intimate connection with the President. In May 1861 Sumner and the President went for an evening drive. The Senator told the President that he was right in his current policy of doing nothing about slavery, but he warned him that he should be ready to strike when the moment came. After the disaster at Bull Run in July, Sumner went to the White House and until midnight he discussed emancipation with Lincoln. He told Lincoln that the moment had come. "Of this I have no doubt," he exclaimed. The President could not agree.[30]

Sumner was not discouraged. He felt that it was his duty to keep the matter before the President. He continued to press the President. On December 27 he had a long interview with Lincoln and was delighted with the outcome. He wrote Governor John A. Andrew urging him to "keep Massachusetts ahead as she has always been. . . . Let the doctrine of Emancipation be proclaimed as an essential and happy agency in subduing a wicked rebellion. In this way you will help a majority of the Cabinet, whose opinions on this subject are fixed, and precede the President himself by a few weeks. He tells me that I am ahead of him only a month or six weeks."[31] Sumner had to wait much longer for favorable action by the President.

Sumner then turned to Congress. On May 26, he offered a resolution that was never acted on. In it he called on Southerners of all colors to cease supporting the rebels and asked the United States government to "maintain all such loyal people, without distinction of color, in their rights as men, according to the principles of the Declaration of Independence." On July 4, 1862, he was back at the White House with a tempting challenge to the President. "You can make this day more sacred and more historic than the Continental Congress." On this occasion the President did not confide to Sumner that he was moving swiftly toward an emancipation policy. He said, simply, "I would do it if I were not afraid that half the officers would fling down their arms and three more states would rise." This greatly distressed Sumner. "He is hard to move. He is honest but inexperienced," Sumner declared in a letter to the English reformer John Bright. Later he told a Massachusetts audience, "Had Emancipation been spoken at this time I cannot doubt that the salvation of our country would have begun thus earlier."[32]

Among the abolitionists none more than the black leader Frederick Douglass pressed on President Lincoln the necessity of converting the war into a crusade against slavery. In the columns of his paper, on the platform, and in letters to friends at home and abroad he contended that the "Union cause would never prosper till the war assumed an Anti-Slavery attitude, and the Negro was enlisted on the loyal side." In an article, "How to End the War," published in May 1861, Douglass pleaded for the use of blacks as soldiers who would "march into the South and raise the banner of Emancipation among the slaves."[33] To a large audience at Cooper Union in New York he set forth his views in

February 1862. He called attention to the government's "uncertainty and vacillation and hesitation in grappling with the great question of the war—slavery." Over the bleeding back of the enslaved blacks, the American nation was destined to "learn lessons of liberty that could be learned in no other way."[34]

As the war moved into its second year, the pressure on the President to free the slaves increased. On June 20, 1862, a delegation of Progressive Friends called on him and presented a memorial praying for the emancipation of the slaves. The resolutions had been adopted at their annual meeting. Lincoln told them that "if a decree of emancipation could abolish slavery, John Brown would have done the work effectually. Such a decree surely could not be more binding than the Constitution, and that cannot be enforced in that part of the country now." Oliver Johnson, one of the members of the delegation, said that was true, but that should not prevent him from *trying* to enforce it. Another, William Barnard, told Lincoln that he hoped that under divine guidance, the President might be led to free the slaves "and thus save the nation from destruction."[35]

Other religious groups besieged the President. In July a committee of the Synod of the Reformed Presbyterian Church presented a copy of resolutions on slavery passed by the Synod. On this occasion the President made a brief but courteous reply. He assured the committee that there was no difference between him and them regarding the moral character of the institution of slavery. The problem was how to get rid of it. "Were an individual asked whether he would wish to have a wen on his neck, he could not hesitate as to the reply; but were it asked whether a man who has such a wen should at once be relieved of it by the application of the surgeon's knife, there might be diversity of opinion, perhaps the man might bleed to death, as the result of such an operation."[36]

By this time Lincoln had decided to issue the Emancipation Proclamation at some date still undetermined. He was compelled by circumstances, nevertheless, to continue to give the impression that no decision had been reached. It was *after* he had reached the momentous decision that the most widely publicized demand for emancipation was made. Horace Greeley, the independent, hypercritical editor of the New York *Tribune*, had long been a foe of slavery. Although generally friendly to the Administration, he did not spare the words when he did not approve of its policies. He did not agree with Lincoln's view that emancipation would hurt the Union cause, and on August 20, 1862, he told him so in a moving editorial, "The Prayer of Twenty Millions."

Many of Lincoln's supporters, Greeley told the President, were "sorely disappointed and deeply pained by the policy you seem to be pursuing with regard to the slaves of rebels. . . . We think you are strangely and disastrously remiss in the discharge of your official and imperative duty with regard to the emancipating provisions of the new Confiscation Act." This act, Greeley said, proposed to fight slavery with liberty and to punish treason; but for some strange reason the President treated the traitors with tenderness "to the prejudice of the dearest rights of loyal men. . . . It is the duty of a Government so wantonly, wickedly assailed by Rebellion as ours has been to oppose force in a defiant, dauntless spirit. It cannot afford to temporize with traitors nor semi-traitors." Greeley observed that the generals who had habitually disregarded the Confiscation Act had not been rebuked by the President but that he had hastily annulled the Frémont and Hunter proclamations favoring emancipation. "As one of the millions who would gladly have avoided this struggle at any sacrifice but that of Principle and Honor, but who now feel that the triumph of the Union is indispensable not only to the existence of our country, but to the well-being of mankind, I entreat you to render a hearty and unequivocal obedience to the law of the land."[37]

Lincoln could not ignore Greeley's biting criticism. The *Tribune* was widely read and greatly respected; and its editor was one of the most ardent supporters of the Union cause. In a reply, which Greeley printed on August 25, the President said that he would not undertake to refute any of Greeley's statements he knew to be erroneous or to argue against any inferences that he believed to be falsely drawn. "If there be perceptible in it an impatient and dictatorial tone, I waive it in deference to an old friend, whose heart I have always supposed to be right." Lincoln then proceeded briefly to state the policy that he was pursuing in words that are among the best known of all his utterances.

> *My paramount object in this struggle* is *to save the Union, and is* not *either to save or to destroy slavery. If I could save the Union without freeing* any *slave I would do it, and if I could save it by freeing* all *the slaves I would do it; and if I could save it by freeing some and leaving others alone I would also do that. What I do about slavery, and the colored race, I do because I believe it helps to save the Union; and what I forbear, I forbear because I do* not *believe it would help save the Union. . . . I shall try to correct errors when shown to be errors; and I shall adopt new views so fast as they shall appear to be true views.*

> *I have here stated my purpose according to my view of* official *duty; and I intend no modification of my oft-expressed* personal *wish that all men every where could be free.*[38]

Greeley could not publish the President's frank reply without restating his own position. In a lengthy response, also published on August 25, Greeley told the President, "I never doubted . . . that you desire, before and above all else, to re-establish the now derided authority . . . of the Republic. I intended to raise only this question—*Do you propose to do this by recognizing, obeying, and enforcing the laws, or by ignoring, disregarding, and in effect denying them?*"[39] Here, both Greeley and Lincoln rested their case.

In the late August days and in the following month—right up to the time he issued the preliminary Emancipation Proclamation—Lincoln listened patiently to those who pressed him to free the slaves. On August 24 he had a lengthy talk with Orestes Brownson, the New England reformer, who was later to describe him as "wrong-headed" and "ill-deserving of the sobriquet of Honest." Lincoln apparently gave him no intimation that he would soon issue the Proclamation. If he had, it would not have satisfied the uncompromising Brownson.

One of the most imposing antislavery delegations called on the President on September 13. Lincoln had spent the night at Soldiers' Home and while riding to the White House that morning he had sprained his wrist while checking his runaway horse. Although in great pain he received the delegation from Chicago, Christians of all denominations. They presented him a memorial in favor of national emancipation that had been adopted at a public meeting in Chicago on September 7. They also presented a memorial in German signed by German citizens of Chicago. The President assured them that he had given much thought to the question of emancipation and indicated that the pressures on him were enormous. "I am approached with the most opposite opinions and advice, and that by religious men, who are equally certain that they represent the Divine will. I am sure that either the one or the other class is mistaken in that belief, and perhaps in some respects both." He told them of an incident that occurred a few days earlier. Four prominent men from New York called on him regarding some business connected with the war. Before they left two of them earnestly requested the President to proclaim general emancipation, whereupon the other two at once attacked them!

Lincoln then asked the men from Chicago what good would a proclamation of emancipation do. "I do not want to issue a document that the whole world will see must necessarily be inoperative, like the Pope's bull against the comet! Would *my word* free the slaves, when I cannot even enforce the Constitution in the rebel states?" He expressed other doubts. What should be done with the slaves if they were freed? How could the Union feed and care for them? Lincoln said that he saw no legal or constitutional objections to a proclamation of emancipation, for as commander-in-chief he had a right "to take any measure which may best subdue the enemy." The delegation argued that nothing could be lost by proclaiming emancipation, even if it could not now be enforced. It would facilitate the prosecution of the war and secure the sympathy of Europe and the whole civilized world.

In concluding the interview that had lasted for an hour, the President sought to console his visitors. He said that he hoped he had not been misunderstood because he had outlined the difficulties connected with issuing a proclamation to free the slaves. "I have not decided against a proclamation of liberty to the slaves, but hold the matter under advisement." He assured them that the matter was on his mind, day and night, "more than any other."[40]

2 The Decision and the Writing

T he road that led to the issuing of the Preliminary
Emancipation Proclamation was a long and difficult
one. It was marked by an incredible amount of pressure on
Abraham Lincoln, pressure that began the day Sumter fell
and that did not relent until his decision was announced on
September 22, 1862. It is not possible to weigh the effects
of the pressures created by hardheaded generals who
would set slaves free in order to break the back of the Confederacy. One cannot know what impressions the procession of the Charles Sumners, the Orestes Brownsons, and
the religious deputations made on the President as they
came by day and by night to tell him what he should do
about slavery. Did a Greeley editorial or a Douglass speech
sway him? One cannot know the answers to these questions, for Lincoln, the only one who could do so, never gave
the answers. He was doubtlessly impressed by all argu-
ments that were advanced, and he took all of them "under
advisement." But the final decision was his.

Lincoln needed no convincing that slavery was wrong,
and he had been determined for many years to strike a blow
for freedom if the opportunity ever came his way. As a
young man he told a New Orleans group in 1831, "If I ever

get a chance to hit that thing, I'll hit it hard."[1] He fully appreciated, moreover, the disastrous effect of slavery on national development and on the national character. He told a Cincinnati audience in 1842 that "Slavery and oppression must cease, or American liberty must perish."[2]

Lincoln was irritated by any suggestion that he was "soft" on the question of slavery. "I am naturally anti-slavery," he wrote a friend shortly after the beginning of his second term. "If slavery is not wrong, nothing is wrong. . . . And yet I have never understood that the Presidency conferred upon me an unrestricted right to act officially on this judgment and feeling. . . . And I aver that to this day [April 4, 1864] I have done no official act in mere deference to my abstract judgment and feeling on slavery."[3]

Thus Lincoln was troubled by unanswered questions regarding the legality as well as the effect of emancipation on the course of the war and on the peace and well-being of the country. Who could know if the soldiers of Kentucky would lay down their arms if Lincoln set the slaves free? Greeley replied, "Let them do it. The cause of Union will be stronger, if Kentucky should secede with the rest, than it is now." It was not quite so simple, when one had the responsibility for shaping the course of the war and preserving the life of the Union. What would happen to the blacks once they are free? Who would take care of them? These were questions that Lincoln asked over and over. Frederick Douglass, the runaway slave who had been a resounding success on two continents, had the answer. "Let them take care of themselves, as others do." If the black man could take care of his master and mistress, he could take care of himself. Should the freed blacks be allowed to remain in the United States? "Yes," Douglass replied, "they wouldn't take up more room than they do now." Facile, even witty answers were not enough for the troubled Lincoln.

Since Lincoln was quite certain that sooner or later, in war or in peace, the slaves would be free, he gave much attention to what should be done with them. "You and we are different races," he told a group of blacks in August 1862. "Whether it is right or wrong I need not discuss, but this physical difference is a great disadvantage to us both, as I think your race suffer very greatly, many of them by living among us, while ours suffer from your presence. In a word we suffer on each side. If this be admitted, it affords a reason at least why we should be separated."[4] Freedom called for colonization, Lincoln felt; and it seemed to occupy his attention about as much as any single matter during the first two years of the war.

As Lincoln moved toward a policy of emancipation, his interest in colonizing blacks in some other parts of the world quickened. Indeed, it is almost possible to measure his approach to emancipation by studying the increasing intensity of his efforts to formulate a feasible program of colonization. In 1854 he said that his first impulse "would be to free all the slaves and send them back to Liberia, to their own native land." In his first annual message he proposed colonization for blacks freed in the course of the war. He urged colonization for the slaves of the District of Columbia when they were freed in April 1862. He spearheaded the legislation in July 1862 that appropriated a half million dollars to colonize slaves of disloyal masters.

When Lincoln met the group of blacks in August 1862, and talked to them about colonization, he had already decided to issue the Proclamation. This very decision seemed to make him all the more anxious about colonization. He asked them to give serious consideration to the idea of colonizing in Central America. The blacks showed little enthusiasm for the proposal. In the following two weeks he discussed colonization in Chiriqui, a province in Panama, with several individuals and with members of the Cabinet. At the end of the month he decided to abandon the project because of lack of support. He was not altogether discouraged, and for the next several months he continued his vain attempts to gain support for colonization.

Early in 1862 Lincoln reached the decision that either he or Congress should emancipate the slaves. By March he had composed the draft of a special message to Congress recommending compensated emancipation. He read it to Senator Sumner, who was not enthusiastic about it because it called for gradual emancipation. Neither Congress nor the Delaware leaders upon whom he urged compensated emancipation were any more enthusiastic than Sumner. While Congress passed a resolution embodying the President's recommendations, it made no serious attempt to implement them.

Lincoln later admitted his awareness of pressures, but he never admitted the effect of them on his decision. He said that he forbade Frémont's and Hunter's attempts at military emancipation because he did not then think it an indispensable necessity. When the border states declined his appeal to accept compensated emancipation, he was driven to the "alternative of either surrendering the Union, and with it, the Constitution, or of laying a strong hand upon the colored element."[5] He chose the latter. In doing so he hoped for greater gain than loss, but of this he was not entirely confident.

The best evidence supports the view that it was in the late spring of 1862 that the President decided to issue a proclamation freeing the slaves. "Things had gone on from bad to worse," he said, "until I felt that we had reached the end of our rope on the plan of operations we had been pursuing; that we had about played our last card, and must change our tactics, or lose the game!" It was then that he "determined on the adoption of the emancipation policy; and without consultation with, or knowledge of the Cabinet, I prepared the original draft of the proclamation. . . ."[6]

Lincoln was a frequent visitor to the telegraph room of the War Department. He went there almost daily to receive the reports of the progress of the war and to get away from the turmoil and distraction of the White House, where he had no privacy. Thomas T. Eckert, who was in charge of the telegraph office, was understanding and unobtrusive. Lincoln usually sat at Eckert's desk while at the telegraph office. Early one June morning, Lincoln dropped into the office and asked Eckert for some paper on which to write something special. He sat down and began to write. "He would look out of the window a while," Eckert later reported, "and then put his pen to paper, but he did not write much at once. He would study between times and when he had made up his mind he would put down a line or two, and then sit quiet for a few minutes. After a time he would resume his writing. . . ."

On that first day Lincoln did not fill one sheet of the paper Eckert had given him. When he left he asked Eckert to keep what he had written and not to show it to anyone. On the following day when he returned, he asked for the paper, which Eckert kept in a locked desk; and he began to write. "This he did every day for several weeks." On some days he did not write more than a line or two, and Eckert observed that he had put question marks in the margin. Each day he would read over what he had written and revise it, "studying carefully each sentence." Eckert later said that he did not know what the President was writing until he had finished the draft. Then, for the first time, he told Eckert that he had been writing an order "giving freedom to the slaves in the South for the purpose of hastening the end of the war." He then explained that he had been able to work more quietly and could better command his thoughts at the telegraph office than at the White House, where he was frequently interrupted.[7]

Within the next few weeks Lincoln widened the circle of confidants with whom he discussed the Proclamation. He had many talks with Stanton, his Secretary of War, about the possible use of blacks as soldiers. Stanton had the distinct impression that Lincoln was planning to emancipate the slaves at an early date. On May 28 he predicted to Senator Sumner that a decree of emancipation would be issued within two months. Although Lincoln was as yet unwilling to arm the slaves, he began to discuss with his advisers the matter of their emancipation *and* their arming. Stanton, an ardent protagonist of both propositions, seemed to be more optimistic as spring gave way to summer in 1862.

On June 18, 1862, the President had a busy day. He received many visitors and, as usual, he fretted over reports of the activity or inactivity of Union troops. To General Henry W. Halleck at Corinth, Mississippi, he sent a message inquiring about the progress of the proposed expedition toward East Tennessee. To McClellan he sent a curt message saying that he could better dispose of things if he knew about what day McClellan could attack Richmond.[8] Things, indeed, seemed to be going from bad to worse. To get away from it all the President had his horse saddled and, with Vice-President Hannibal Hamlin, rode out to the Soldiers' Home for his evening meal. After dinner the two men retired to the library and talked behind locked doors. According to Hamlin the President began the conversation by saying, "Mr. Hamlin, you have been repeatedly urging me to issue a proclamation of emancipation freeing the slaves. I have concluded to yield to your advice in the matter and that of other friends,—at the same time, as I may say, following my own judgment. Now listen to me as I read this paper. We will correct it together as I go on."

The President then opened a drawer in his desk and took out the draft of the Proclamation. He read it slowly, during which time the Vice-President made no interruptions. When he had finished, Hamlin said that he had no criticism. Lincoln could hardly believe that Hamlin regarded the document as perfect. "At least you can make some suggestions," Lincoln urged. Finally, Hamlin reported, he did make "three suggestions, two of which Mr. Lincoln accepted." He declined to make known what his suggestions were, insisting that the Emancipation Proclamation was the President's "own act, and no one else can claim any credit whatever in connection with it."[9]

The death of young James Hutchison Stanton, Stanton's infant son, occurred at about the same time in July, 1862, as McClellan's retreat from Richmond. Lincoln was grieved by both events, and his depressed state was apparent to his associates. He invited the Secretary of the Navy, Gideon

Welles, and the Secretary of State, William H. Seward, to accompany him in the Presidential carriage to the infant's funeral. It was during this ride, on July 13, that Lincoln first mentioned his proposed emancipation proclamation to these highly placed advisers. The President "dwelt earnestly on the gravity, importance, and delicacy of the movement, said he had given it much thought and had about come to the conclusion that it was a military necessity absolutely essential for the salvation of the Union, that we must free the slaves or be ourselves subdued. . . ."

Welles recorded in his diary that Lincoln told them that this was the first time that he had mentioned the subject to anyone. The President invited the two men to state frankly how the proposition struck them. Seward, never lacking a response, said that the subject involved consequences so vast and momentous that he wished more time for mature reflection before giving a decisive answer. His offhand opinion, however, was that the measure was "perfectly justifiable" and perhaps might be expedient and necessary. Welles concurred in this view.

During the ride of some two or three miles beyond Georgetown the three men returned to the subject several times. When they returned to the city the President asked Seward and Welles, as they took their leave, to give the matter their "specific and deliberate attention." As for himself he was firm in his conviction that something must be done.[10]

It was hardly accurate to say that Lincoln had never discussed the matter with anyone. One wonders if Welles's memory was playing tricks on him or if the President's agitated state caused him to speak inaccurately. It was, however, accurate for Welles to declare that it was a new departure for the President to state categorically that he intended to emancipate the slaves. Heretofore, as Welles stated, whenever the matter arose, the President had been "prompt and emphatic in denouncing any interference by the General Government with the subject." The reverses before Richmond and the formidable power and dimensions of the rebellion were forcing the Administration to adopt extraordinary measures to preserve the Union. The proposed emancipation of the slaves fell into the category of extraordinary measures.

The formal solicitation of advice from the Cabinet came at the meeting on July 22, a scarce ten days after the momentous discussion during the funeral ride. When the meeting was called to order, all members were present except Montgomery Blair, the Postmaster General, who arrived during the meeting. The President informed the Cabinet that he had resolved to issue a proclamation emancipating the slaves. His decision in the matter was firm, he assured them. He therefore had called them together to inform them and to solicit their suggestions regarding language and timing.

The President then proceeded to read the following document:*

In pursuance of the sixth section of the act of Congress entitled "An act to suppress insurrection and to punish treason and rebellion, to seize and confiscate property of rebels, and for other purposes" Approved July 17, 1862, and which act, and the Joint Resolution explanatory thereof, are herewith published, I, Abraham Lincoln, President of the United States, do hereby proclaim to, and warn all persons within the contemplation of said sixth section to cease participating in, aiding, countenancing, or abetting the existing rebellion, or any rebellion against the government of the United States, and to return to their proper allegiance to the United States, on pain of the forfeitures and seizures, as within and by sixth section provided.

And I hereby make known that it is my purpose, upon the next meeting of congress, to again recommend the adoption of a practical measure for tendering aid to the free choice or rejection, of any and all States which may then be recognizing and sustaining the authority of the United States, and which may then have voluntarily adopted, or thereafter may voluntarily adopt, gradual

*For a reproduction, see the second page of the photo section.

abolishment of slavery within such State or States—that the object is to practically restore, thence forward to be maintain[ed], the constitutional relation between the general government, and each, and all the states, wherein that relation is now suspended, or disturbed; and that, for this object, the war, as it has been, will be, prossecuted. And, as a fit and necessary military measure for effecting this object, I, as Commander-in-Chief of the Army and Navy of the United States, do order and declare that on the first day of January in the year of Our Lord one thousand eight hundred and sixtythree, all persons held as slaves within any state or states, wherein the constitutional authority of the United States shall not then be practically recognized, submitted to, and maintained, shall then, thenceforward, and forever, be free.[11]

There is no known copy of the Proclamation that Lincoln drafted in Eckert's office in the War Department. Perhaps it was similar to the second paragraph of the document the President read to his Cabinet on July 22. The latter document, however, rested largely on the authorization provided by the Confiscation Act of July 17, 1862. One can be certain, therefore, that this draft was written less than five days before the meeting of the Cabinet. It was on two pages of lined note paper, $12^{1/2}$ by $7^{7/8}$ inches and is now in the Library of Congress. The President endorsed the document as the "Emancipation Proclamation as first sketched and shown to the Cabinet in July, 1862."

Upon the completion of the reading a lively discussion ensued. Despite the prior knowledge of some members of the Cabinet that the President was drafting such a document, interest in the Proclamation was high. Doubtless some members could not believe their ears. Since the first paragraph had the backing of law, there was no extensive consideration of this portion of the proclamation.

Edward Bates, the Attorney General, gave unreserved concurrence. Salmon P. Chase, the Secretary of the Treasury, said that the measure went beyond anything he contemplated. He would prefer to permit the generals to arm the blacks and proclaim emancipation locally, as they occupied portions of the Confederacy. Stanton, the Secretary of War, had long urged emancipation and arming of the slaves. He, therefore, favored the President's issuing the proclamation at once. The Postmaster General, Montgomery Blair, thought the proposed action was highly impolitic and would cost the administration the fall elections. This would, of course, have an adverse effect upon the conduct and course of the war, he argued.

The most significant observations were made by the Secretary of State. Seward made it clear that he approved the Proclamation, but he questioned the expediency of its issue "at this juncture." The repeated reverses of the Union army had depressed the public mind. An Emancipation Proclamation issued at this time may be viewed as a "last measure of an exhausted government, a cry for help, the government stretching forth its hands to the Ethiopia, instead of Ethiopia stretching forth her hands to the government."[12] He suggested that the matter be postponed "until you can give it to the country supported by military success, attended by fife and drum and public spirit."[13]

Lincoln was impressed by Seward's argument, but he did not commit himself at the meeting. Later in the afternoon he had his second conference of the day with Francis B. Cutting, an ardent proslavery Democratic lawyer from New York. Despite his views on slavery Cutting was convinced of the necessity of emancipation in order to forestall diplomatic recognition of the Confederacy and to rally the antislavery element behind the war. He expressed these views fully to Lincoln during the first interview. When the two men met after the Cabinet meeting Lincoln told Cutting that he intended to issue the proclamation the following day, July 23.

On the same day Blair sent the President a lengthy statement reaffirming his objection to the Proclamation on political grounds. He insisted that there was no public sentiment in the North, "even among extreme men which now demands the proposed measure." He argued that it would

endanger the Administration's power in Congress and hand
to those opposed to the war the control of the next House of
Representatives.[14]

That evening Thurlow Weed, the remarkably astute political leader from New York, met with the President. He
argued for postponement, not to reinforce Blair's argu-
ments, but in support of Seward's views. He told Lincoln
that the Proclamation could not be enforced, and its issuance at that time would be folly. Apparently, Lincoln
agreed. Two days later he issued the "Proclamation of the
Act to Suppress Insurrection," which was the first paragraph of the document he had read to the Cabinet. Presidential emancipation would wait—not for the fall elections
but for a Union victory.

Lincoln did not merely file away the Proclamation for
"future use." It remained constantly in his thoughts; and if
he was ever disposed to neglect the matter, the constant
pressure by Greeley and the others would have made this
impossible.

The next two months were difficult for Lincoln. The
Proclamation was prepared, but the propitious moment for
its issuance seemed never to come. The public, unaware of
his plans, continued to urge an emancipation policy upon
him. Military leaders, including Stanton, wanted Lincoln to
arm the slaves. If Stanton did not press the President with
greater zeal, he could not forget the manner in which Lincoln countermanded the actions of Hunter, Frémont, and
the others. Stanton was among those who believed that
armed slaves would accelerate the arrival of the proper
moment to issue the Emancipation Proclamation. Lincoln
could not agree; and he waited.

In the meetings of the Cabinet in August emancipation
remained a subject of interest and discussion. On August 3
Chase urged the President to assure freedom for the slaves
in the seceded states on condition of loyalty.[15] During those
days that seemed an eternity, unknowing men and women
chastised Lincoln for not reaching a decision on emancipa-

tion. He was always gracious and patient with all armchair emancipators and military strategists. He continued to wait, but he was becoming more anxious.

At the end of August, Second Bull Run was fought; and the Union troops were repulsed almost as sharply as they had been at First Bull Run thirteen months earlier. After this disaster the Union cause was at a most critical juncture. Even the capital was once more in danger. Lee was determined to capitalize on the victory and take the fight to the enemy. Early in September he crossed the Potomac near Leesburg and, on the seventh of September, occupied Frederick, Maryland.

Panic struck the entire North as news of Lee's movements spread. Some feared that Washington, Baltimore, and Philadelphia would fall. Lincoln fretted, and spent more time than usual at the War Department telegraph office. He must keep in touch with McClellan, now in command of the forces destined to repel Lee. After a sleepless night on September 11 he wired McClellan at 4 A.M., "How does it look now?" Things never looked too good to McClellan, and he remained diffident about advancing against Lee. But he could have replied that things were looking better. A Union private had discovered Lee's orders revealing the disposition of his forces, and had turned them over to McClellan. But the wary, hesitant leader lost his chances of destroying Lee's army because, characteristically, he overestimated enemy strength and power.

Lee's forces were inferior to McClellan's, and Lee knew it. With inadequate forces to push his invasion to the North, Lee resolved to withdraw across the Potomac into Virginia. At long last, however, McClellan made the attack at Antietam Creek, near Sharpsburg, on September 17. For fourteen hours the armies fought, and at the close of the day more than twenty thousand Union and Confederate soldiers lay dead and wounded. It was the heaviest engagement in American history up to that time. McClellan's claim of victory was disputed, but it could not be denied that

Lee's offensive had been checked. On the following day Lee recrossed the Potomac and escaped the crushing blow that McClellan could have delivered had he pursued the intrepid Confederate leader. It was this failure to pursue the enemy that caused Lincoln to refer to McClellan's army as "the general's bodyguard."

Although Lincoln was disappointed in the outcome of Antietam it gave him the success he had long sought. Even on the evening of September 17, sensing victory, he worked on the final draft of the preliminary Emancipation Proclamation in the quiet of Soldiers' Home. On Saturday, the twentieth, he returned to the White House, ready to summon the Cabinet on Monday and tell his official family of his decision to issue the Proclamation immediately. On Sunday morning he carefully rewrote the document that was the culmination of months of work and worry.[16]

Once Lincoln made up his mind to issue the Proclamation, he lost no time in informing his Cabinet of his decision. Early on Monday morning he summoned the members of the Cabinet to the White House. By this time Washington was rife with rumors of an impending Proclamation. Every member of the Cabinet had known since July that sooner or later Lincoln would summon them and tell them that the time had come. After the President had finished his reading from Artemus Ward's new book, they could hardly have been surprised when he began to read his Proclamation. They listened attentively, doubtless sensing the enormous significance of the step the President was taking not only for the course of the war but also for the character and composition of the American social order.

After the President had read the draft of the Proclamation, he invited comments, making it clear that the decision and the consequences were his. There ensued a "long and earnest" discussion in which the President participated. Seward suggested one or two unimportant emendations that were approved. The document was then given to

Seward to publish on the following day. Blair, ever political-minded and lukewarm on the slavery question, said that while he approved the principle of emancipation he did not concur in the expediency of the measure. He was convinced that the Emancipation Proclamation would drive the border slave states into the Confederacy. He thought, too, that certain elements in the free states that were opposed to the Administration would use the measure as a club with which to fight the party in power.[17]

The entire Cabinet entered into a general discussion of the question of the authority that the government possessed to set the slaves free. Some thought the government did not have the authority and that special legislation should be enacted before the step was taken. The President was convinced that under his war powers he had the authority to emancipate the slaves, and he had no intention of seeking further Congressional approval. Stanton remained silent, but as a strong advocate of the use of black troops and as a vigorous opponent of compensated emancipation he was undoubtedly disappointed. Chase was willing to take the document as written, although he would have approached the matter somewhat differently. This was not the first or the last time that he and the President would differ in their approaches. As usual the President had his way.

The Proclamation of September 22, 1862, commonly referred to as the "Preliminary Emancipation Proclamation," was based firmly on legislative and executive authority. It referred to the act of Congress of March 13, 1862, that prohibited officers from aiding in the capture or return of runaway slaves of disloyal masters. And it invoked the well-known Confiscation Act of July 17, 1862, that gave freedom to fugitive, captured, and abandoned slaves of rebels. Obedience to the provisions of these acts would itself result in the emancipation of numerous slaves. Proper construction and enforcement of these acts would result in a considerable amount of emancipation by act of Congress.

As Commander-in-Chief of the Army and Navy, Lincoln referred to his military powers as the source of *his* authority to emancipate the slaves. This power was to be used to prosecute the war in order to restore the Union. Setting the slaves free had become an important means of accomplishing this end. He hoped, finally, to bring about legislative and executive cooperation with a view to developing a plan of emancipation in states that were not in rebellion and to colonize blacks in Africa or elsewhere.

The significant feature of the proclamation was the provision that called for the emancipation of slaves on January 1, 1863, in those states or parts of states that were then in rebellion against the United States. The clear implication was that if states or portions of states were not in rebellion on January 1, 1863, the Proclamation would not apply to them. Apparently, in such areas the President would seek to develop some plan of voluntary immediate or gradual emancipation. It was this provision that was to provoke the greatest amount of reaction in the months that followed.

The body of the Preliminary Emancipation Proclamation is in Lincoln's own hand, the penciled additions in the hand of the Secretary of State, and the final beginning and ending in the hand of the chief clerk. The document was presented by the President to the Albany Army Relief Bazaar held in February and March, 1864. Gerrit Smith, the abolitionist leader, purchased it for $1000 and gave it to the United States Sanitary Commission. In April 1865, the New York Legislature appropriated $1000 for its purchase and it was placed in the State Library. It is still in the possession of the New York State Library. The text, with the Lincoln and Seward emendations, follows:*

BY THE PRESIDENT OF THE
UNITED STATES OF AMERICA

A Proclamation.

I, Abraham Lincoln, President of the United States of America, and Commander-in-Chief of the Army and Navy thereof, do hereby proclaim and declare that here-

*For a reproduction of this document, see the end of the photo section.

after, as heretofore, the war will be prossecuted for the object of practically restoring the constitutional relation between the United States, and each of the states, and the people thereof, in which states that relation is, or may be suspended, or disturbed.

That it is my purpose upon the next meeting of Congress to again recommend the adoption of a practical measure tendering pecuniary aid to the free acceptance or rejection of all slave-states, so called, the people whereof may not then be in rebellion against the United States, and which states may then have voluntarily adopted, or thereafter may voluntarily adopt, immediate or gradual abolishment of slavery within their respective limits; and that the effort to colonize persons of African descent [with their consent]ª upon this continent, or elsewhere, [with the previously obtained consent of the Governments existing there]ª will be continued.

That on the first day of January in the year of our Lord, one thousand eight hundred and sixty-three, all persons held as slaves within any state, or designated part of a state, the people whereof shall be in rebellion against the United States shall be then, thenceforward, and forever free; and the executive government of the United States [including the military and naval authority thereof]ᵇ will recognize [and maintain the freedom of]ᵇ such persons, and will do no act or acts to repress such persons, or any of them, in any efforts they may make for their actual freedom.

That the executive will, on the first day of January aforesaid, by proclamation, designate the States, and parts of states, if any, in which the people thereof respectively, shall then be in rebellion against the United States; and the fact that any state, or the people thereof shall, on that day be, in good faith represented in the Congress of the United States, by members chosen thereto, at elections wherein a majority of the qualified voters of such state shall have participated, shall, in the absence of strong countervailing testimony, be deemed conclusive evidence that such state and the people thereof, are not then in rebellion against the United States.

That attention is hereby called to an Act of Congress entitled "An act to make an additional Article of War"

ª in Seward's hand
ᵇ in Lincoln's hand

approved March 13, 1862, and which act is in the words and figure following:[c]

Be it enacted by the Senate and House of Representatives of the United States of America in Congress assembled, *That hereafter the following shall be promulgated as an additional article of war for the government of the army of the United States, and shall be obeyed and observed as such:*

Article—.All officers or persons in the military or naval service of the United States are prohibited from employing any of the forces under their respective commands for the purpose of returning fugitives from service or labor, who may have escaped from any persons to whom such service or labor is claimed to be due, and any officer who shall be found guilty by a court-martial of violating this article shall be dismissed from the service.

Sec. 2. And be it further enacted, *That this act shall take effect from and after its passage.*

Also to the ninth and tenth sections of an act entitled, "An Act to suppress Insurrection, to punish Treason and Rebellion, to seize and confiscate property of rebels, and for other purposes," approved July 17, 1862, and which sections are in the words and figures following:[d]

Sec. 9. And be it further enacted, *That all slaves of persons who shall hereafter be engaged in rebellion against the government of the United States, or who shall in any way give aid or comfort thereto, escaping from such persons and taking refuge within the lines of the army; and all slaves captured from such persons or deserted by them and coming under the control of the government of the United States; and all slaves of such persons found on (or) being within any place occupied by rebel forces and afterwards occupied by the forces of the United States, shall be deemed captives of war, and shall be forever free of their servitude and not again held as slaves.*

[c] A clipping from the official printing was inserted at this point.
[d] Another clipping from the official printing was inserted at this point.

Sec. 10. And be it further enacted, *That no slave escaping into any State, territory, or the District of Columbia, from any other State, shall be delivered up, or in any way impeded or hindered of his liberty, except for crime, or some offence against the laws, unless the person claiming such fugitive shall first make oath that the person to whom the labor or service of such fugitive is alleged to be due is his lawful owner, and has not borne arms against the United States in the present rebellion, nor in any way given aid and comfort thereto; and no person engaged in the military or naval service of the United States shall, under any pretence whatever, assume to decide on the validity of the claim of any person to the service or labor of any other person, or surrender up any such person to the claimant, on pain of being dismissed from the service.*

And I do hereby enjoin upon and order all persons engaged in the military and naval service of the United States to observe, obey, and enforce within their respective spheres of service, the act, and sections above recited.

And the executive will in due time recommend that all citizens of the United States who shall have remained loyal thereto throughout the rebellion shall (upon the restoration of the constitutional relation between the United States, and their respective states, and people, if that relation shall have been suspended or disturbed) be compensated for all losses by acts of the United States, including the loss of slaves.

In witness whereof, I have hereunto set my hand, and caused the seal of the United States to be affixed.

Done at the City of Washington, this twenty second day of September, in the year of our Lord, one thousand, eight hundred and sixty two, and sixty two, [sic] and of the Independence of the United States, the eighty seventh.

ABRAHAM LINCOLN
By the President
WILLIAM H. SEWARD
Secretary of State.

This was, in a very real sense, the President's own Proclamation. The composition of it began in the War Department's telegraph office in June and continued down through those September days at Soldiers' Home and at the White House the day before the Cabinet meeting. Hamlin, Welles, and Seward gave him no substantive assistance in his private consultations with them. The assistance offered by the Cabinet was essentially of an editorial nature. Even if members of the Cabinet had ideas and approaches that were substantially different from those of Lincoln's, he tended to discourage them from expressing them. If the President claimed for himself the responsibility for making the decision and for reaping the consequences, there was little the Cabinet could do.

To be sure Chase said that he would have approached the matter somewhat differently, but he did not press the point with any vigor in the Cabinet. Meanwhile he had managed to convey the impression among his followers that his influence on the President's emancipation policy was greater than it actually was. In Ohio a group of blacks passed a vote of thanks for the way in which Chase had fulfilled his duties toward the oppressed "as a member of President Lincoln's Cabinet."[18] Another supporter was even more enthusiastic. On October 1, 1862, John Livingston wrote Chase, "The government is now on your platform, and it is right. Everything I have, even to life itself, is now at the disposal of the authorities if necessary to carry out the views expressed by you and adopted by the President."[19] Thus, some of the followers of Chase failed to give the President full credit for the decision and the writing of the Proclamation. In other quarters the credit and the blame were laid at the President's door.

3 The Hundred Days

The historic meeting of the Cabinet was hardly over on September 22, 1862, before the printing and distribution of the Preliminary Proclamation had begun. That afternoon and evening the employees of the Government Printing Office worked late and prepared copies for distribution to the press and government agencies. Seward, the Secretary of State, ordered copies that were to go, along with a circular, to the numerous diplomatic posts of the United States in foreign countries. For the War Department, fifteen thousand copies of General Orders, number 139, dated September 24, 1862, and including the Proclamation, were printed and readied for distribution among the various military commanders and their troops.[1] The Preliminary Proclamation had been long coming. But once the decision was made and the document signed, there was no delay in presenting it to the world.

On the two days following the signing of the Preliminary Proclamation, the text of the document was printed in newspapers throughout the country. It appeared in the Washington *National Republican* on September 23, and in papers in New York, Boston, and Cincinnati on the same day. Within a week it was the subject of serious and critical discussion on the part of editors, reformers, politicians, slaves, soldiers, and Confederate leaders.

The first public reaction was a most favorable one. On September 22, the very day that the contents of the Proclamation were disclosed, a group of Washington citizens announced that they would serenade the President on the following day. At the appointed hour a large crowd, accompanied by a band, appeared and shouted for the President. Soon he appeared, with John Hay, his secretary, at his side. When he said that he had not been informed why the group was honoring him, the people shouted, "It is because of the Proclamation." After some bantering with the crowd, the President said,

> *What I did I did after full deliberation and under a very heavy and solemn sense of responsibility. (Cries of "Good," "God bless you," and applause.) I can only trust in God that I made no mistake. (Cries of "No.") I shall make no attempt on this occasion to sustain what I have done or said by any argument. It's now for the country and the world to pass judgment on it and may be take action upon it.[2]*

When the President had finished, loud cheers went up from the crowd. This continued until he had withdrawn into the White House. Then, the crowd paraded to the residence of Chase, the Secretary of the Treasury, who obliged them with remarks. Chase said that the Proclamation marked the "dawn of a new era; and although the act was performed from an imperative sense of duty . . . it is nevertheless, though baptised in blood, an act of humanity and justice which the latest generation will celebrate." Cassius Clay, soon to return to his post as Minister to Russia, added that anyone who would not stand by the Proclamation was a traitor. The evening ended on a somewhat unhappy note. When the crowd called on Attorney General Bates, he declared that God would see the country through. But when asked to remark on the Proclamation, he declined, saying, "I shall not discuss the acts of the Cabinet, of which I am a member, or of the President, who is my superior."

Two other groups called on the President during that first week and congratulated him for issuing the Proclamation. One was a committee from the Congregational Churches of New York, headed by Henry Ward Beecher. A stanch abolitionist and a brother of the author of *Uncle Tom's Cabin*, Beecher was particularly delighted to hand over to the President a set of resolutions that placed unqualified endorsement on the President's action. The other was a delegation of twelve loyal governors who had been meeting in Altoona, Pennsylvania. Speaking for his colleagues, Governor John A. Andrew of Massachusetts congratulated the President upon the Proclamation, "believing it will do good as a measure of justice and sound policy."[3] Only Governor Augustus Bradford of Maryland was unwilling to give his official sanction since he was not certain of the expediency of the Proclamation.[4] Governor Frederick Holbrook of Vermont, who was not present at the conference of governors, told his legislature that the Proclamation would be accepted and sustained by all loyal men.[5]

From two sources, widely separated by political commitments as well as by distance, the President was encouraged in what he had done. Ohio's Democratic Governor David Tod, in a speech on October 6 declared that he cordially endorsed "every word and syllable of it." It was perfectly timed, he said, adding that Lincoln "should be praised for forbearance, for acting as President of South Carolina as well as Ohio."[6] On the same day, in a speech in Boston, Charles Sumner gave the Proclamation his blessing. "Thank God," he exulted, "the skies are brighter and the air is purer, now that slavery has been handed over to judgment." He said that he accepted the compromise without note or comment. "It is enough for me that in the exercise of the war power, it strikes at the origin and mainspring of this Rebellion, for I have never concealed the conviction that it mattered little where we struck slavery."[7]

Frederick Douglass, the best known and most influential black in the country, was greatly encouraged by the Preliminary Proclamation. Lincoln's reply to Greeley's "Prayer of Twenty Millions" had depressed him, while the President's various colonization schemes filled him with despair. At least the emancipation policy was a step in the right direction. He would hope for the best, and he would do his best. In a pamphlet "Slaves' Appeal to Great Britain," prepared shortly after Lincoln's Preliminary Proclamation, Douglass urged England not to recognize the Confederacy. From September 22, 1862, on, the war was "invested with sanctity and England was morally bound to hold aloof from the Confederacy. . . ."[8]

While the loyal governors and Sumner and Douglass were not all the people, it must have been encouraging to Lincoln to learn that such responsible and representative leaders had endorsed the Preliminary Proclamation. If he needed further approval, he could get it from a wide but selected sampling of the press. In the capital the *National Republican* declared that the Proclamation would be read "with far more exciting interest than the details of battles. This Proclamation is the beginning of the end, or rather it is the end. . . . The Proclamation will be received by the loyal States with a perfect *furore* of acclamation. It will lose the President a few latter-day friends, who did not profess to become such until after his election. . . . But it will restore to the President all his old friends, and unite the sound portion of the people in one solid and impregnable mass in support of the Union and the Constitution. . . ."[9]

When the word reached Horace Greeley in New York he seemed, for once, to be at a loss for words. He wrote simply, "It is the beginning of the end of the rebellion; the beginning of the new life of the nation. God bless Abraham Lincoln." On the following day, when he had recovered his usual mastery of words, Greeley wrote a long editorial praising the President for transforming a state "sunk in the semi-barbarism of a medieval age to the light and civilization of the Nineteenth Christian Century." He said that it was a simple statement of a truth to say that "in all ages there has been no act of one man and of one people so sublime as this emancipation of a race—no act so fraught with good for the sons of men in all time to come."[10]

The editor of the New York *Times* struck a similar note. He thought that there had been "no more important and far-reaching document ever issued since the foundation of this Government," than the Proclamation.[11] The editor of the Boston *Evening Transcript* was especially pleased that the President approached the problem deliberately and did not act until necessary. Many would ask what good will it do. In reply to his own question, the editor said, "The enunciation of a principle often, more than that, almost always, precedes its practical application. The announcement of a policy is the plan by which action is to be aroused and governed."[12] A Providence, Rhode Island, editor welcomed the President's action. He had been cautious and conservative, and now the great majority of loyal men were ready for the emancipation.[13]

In Cincinnati an editor was delighted that the Union was no longer willing to protect "the compulsory labor system *which feeds the enemy.*" The Proclamation was an exercise of the rights of war, "a legitimate means of aiding military action."[14] *Harper's Weekly* called the Proclamation a "blessed boom." It was confident that emancipation would spread to the border states and become universal. Liberal views would, in time, permeate society, "and stamp themselves on the mind of the working-class. . . . We do not . . . apprehend any serious opposition at the North to the President's policy, except in circles whose loyalty to the country may well be questioned."[15]

Lincoln was too much of a realist to be enchanted by the burst of enthusiasm that greeted his Preliminary Proclamation in many quarters. There were few in whom he could confide his real feelings. Vice-President Hannibal Hamlin was one. Writing from Bangor, Maine, Hamlin told Lincoln the Proclamation was "the great act of the age. It will prove to be wise in statesmanship as it is patriotic." Lincoln had his doubts, and he expressed them to Hamlin. While he hoped some good would come from the Proclamation, he told the Vice-President that his expectations were "not as sanguine as . . . those of some friends. . . . While commendation in newspapers and by distinguished individuals is all a vain man could wish, the stocks have declined, and troops come forward more slowly than ever. . . . The North responds to the Proclamation sufficiently in breath; but breath alone kills no rebels."[16]

Those who doubted the wisdom or the legality of the Proclamation or who disapproved it outright were as articulate as those who approved it. One of the opponents had visited the President on the day before he wrote the Vice-President, and he doubtless had this interview in mind when he wrote his colleague. Edward Stanly, former Whig Congressman from North Carolina, had been appointed Military Governor of North Carolina on May 26, 1862. During the summer, reports reached Washington that Stanly had prevented the education of black children in North Carolina. While the report was never confirmed, the matter remained unresolved. Consequently Stanly came to Washington in September to confer with Lincoln and Administration leaders.

In talking with Lincoln, Stanly apparently satisfied Lincoln that he was not guilty of the charge of preventing the education of blacks. He made it clear, however, that he was opposed to the Proclamation. Stanly looked upon the war as a struggle to save the Union and nothing more. It was with this understanding that he had agreed to become the Military Governor of North Carolina. He made it clear to Lincoln that he regarded the Proclamation as a "sudden and grave departure from the previous theory of the War." It was now Lincoln's turn to satisfy Stanly. The President declared that the Proclamation had become a civil necessity to prevent the Radicals from openly embarrassing the government in the conduct of the War. The Proclamation thus became an important ingredient in the formula to save the

Union. Apparently Stanly was convinced, for he returned to his post without further complaint. Stanly's words were, perhaps, the first adverse comment on the Proclamation that Lincoln had heard. It was not to be the last.[17]

If Lincoln could read words of unqualified praise in one sector of the American press, he could read words of doubt and disapproval in another. In the capital, the *Star* admitted that it was silent on the Proclamation "simply and plainly for the reason that whatever doubts we may have as to the policy . . . to urge them now that the policy is a foregone conclusion cannot be advantageous to the national cause."[18]

The editor of another Washington paper, the *National Intelligencer*, was not quite so diffident. "With our well-known and oft-repeated views respecting the inutility of such proclamations," he said, "it can hardly be necessary for us to say that, where we expect no good, we shall be only too happy to find that no harm has been done by the present declaration. . . ." He saw little difference, except "in the signatures respectively attached to them," between the Proclamation of General Hunter and that of the President. One was likely to prove as void in practical effect as the other. Since the President had yielded to the pressures of Greeley, Phillips, and the others regarding emancipation, he must be prepared to face further pressures from them as they seek to place some of their group in the Cabinet and in the field.[19]

Prominent among other important papers that were tentative in their attitude toward the Proclamation was the New York *Herald*. In an editorial two days after the Proclamation was issued the editor said, "We accept this proclamation . . . not as that of an armed crusade against African slavery, but as a peace offering to our loyal border slave states, and as a liberal warning to our revolted states, in order to save their local institutions by their timely restoration to the Union."[20] The Baltimore *American* doubted that any good would come as a result of the Proclamation. "We do not think anything whatever is to answer in putting down the rebellion except the uttermost vigor in our military and naval movements. . . . We confess that we had rather hear of such movements . . . than to speculate doubtfully upon the effects of the Proclamation. . . ."[21]

The Proclamation came in for its share of downright criticism and opposition in the Northern press. Some editors thought the Proclamation impolitic, others thought it hypocritical, while others regarded it as illegal. "It is not constitutional," the Hartford *Times* declared. "In policy it is wrong, and will work an injury rather than any good to the Union cause." The Boston *Post* said the only purpose of the Proclamation was "to introduce contention where harmony is necessary to our national salvation, and doubt where confidence was gaining ascendancy."[22] The *Herald* of Newburyport, Massachusetts, was especially irritated with Lincoln's decision because the President "knew" that such a measure would divide the North. He not only knew it but had told "the Progressive Quakers that it would lose him fifty thousand men in Kentucky."[23]

Division of the Union was offered as the reason for opposition to the Proclamation by some segments of the business community. After discussing the unconstitutionality of the Proclamation, the editor of the New York *Express* commented that the Proclamation provokes the question among businessmen "when this war is to end, and how is it to end—if that end is to be the destruction of the labour system of the South—cotton, tobacco, rice, sugar, etc.—what our ships freight; what our commission merchants make their profits on, and what supports vast masses of manufacturing labour in the North. . . . What interest has commerce in prosecuting a war upon such destructive and revolutionary principles. . . ." The New York *Journal of Commerce*, likewise distressed over the Proclamation, asserted that "The President does not expect his new policy to be supported by the conservative men of the country, who believe it to be unconstitutional and wrong." It stated that all who believed the Proclamation "to be disastrous in its necessary effects, will unite in the elections which are approaching."[24]

The partisan note that was struck by the editor of the *Journal of Commerce* was doubtless a consideration in the minds of other critics of the Proclamation. Despite lofty protests to the contrary, the vehemence with which the anti-Administration New York *World* attacked the President was strongly partisan. He had "swung loose from the constitutional moorings of his inaugural address. . . . He is fully adrift on the current of radical fanaticism." It said that the Proclamation had been made "in pursuance of that higher law—that is to say, that open defiance of law—which has distinguished the tribe of pestilent abolition agitators from the beginning." It declared that the Union could never be restored without a reversal of the President's action.[25]

No Union supporter could have expected anything but denunciation of the Proclamation from Confederate quarters. The vigor of the Confederate denunciation and the intensity of the resentment must have been of great interest to Union leaders who had to evaluate the various reactions to the Proclamation. The press of the Confederate capital presumably spoke for most of the adherents to the cause of secession. On September 29 the Richmond *Examiner* carried on its front page the full text of the Proclamation, introducing it as "The most important feature of the news from the North." Editorially, the *Examiner* declared, "The Government of the United States has shot its bolt. . . . It will have no effect on the South; its only serious importance is its indication that the North will stop at nothing in prosecuting the War." It was, the editor concluded, a "call for the insurrection of four million slaves, and the inauguration of a reign of hell upon earth!"[26]

The Richmond *Whig* adjudged the Proclamation an important landmark in the history of the War. While it would have no practical consequences in the South, it served to show the stage at which Northern opinion had arrived and to "indicate the views of the situation now held by the Washington government. . . . Its effects will, in no wise, differ from the effects already experienced in those districts of the South which have been subjected to the rule of the enemy. . . . Whenever a Yankee army has appeared practical emancipation has followed." The editor asserted that the Proclamation would have been issued earlier except for fear of arousing opposition in the North and of losing power in the fall elections. The President was pushed into issuing the Proclamation by the abolitionists. It is the "last resort of a defeated, perplexed and desperate government. It is a good sign for the South."[27]

It was left for the Richmond *Enquirer* to level the bitterest denunciation against the Lincoln government. The Proclamation was the "last extremity of wickedness which it was left to our enemy to adopt." The whole course of the people of the North "has been of a character to destroy any possible remains of past sympathies, and to extinguish every pleasurable feeling with which we used to recall the brilliant events that occurred in the period of our association with them. . . . Lincoln has crowned the pyramid of his infamies with an atrocity abhorred of men, and at which even demons should suffer." The editor said that even Lincoln had pretended that he was working for the restoration of the Union. But the Proclamation showed him to be "as black of soul as the vilest of the train whose behests he is obeying. So far as he can do so, he has devoted the Southern Confederacy to the Direst destruction that can befall a people."[28]

On September 30 the Charleston *Mercury* published the text of the Proclamation, and on the following day it published an editorial on the measure. It followed the same general line of the Richmond papers. It called it a "stroke of desperate statesmanship." It hoped that President Davis would respond by calling up men between thirty-five and forty-five.[29] The Arkansas *State Gazette* hoped that it would increase border state support for the South. Meanwhile, it called for acts of retaliation in order to "compel observance of the forms of honor, honesty and decency."[30]

The Southern press devoted much space to reprinting Northern editorials critical of the Proclamation. The Richmond *Whig* carried an editorial by the New York *Albion* denouncing Lincoln's "atrocious proclamation." The New Orleans *Picayune* reprinted the Boston *Post's* statement that the Proclamation dropped Lincoln in the hands of the "radical revolutionary party." The Richmond *Examiner* published the critical comments of the New York papers, the *Herald*, the *World*, and the *Journal of Commerce*.[31]

Two fears ran through Southern editorial comment on the Proclamation. One was the fear of servile insurrection that would be inspired by Lincoln's act. He had ordained it, and it was not for a moment misunderstood in the North or the South, the Richmond *Enquirer* screamed.[32] The Charleston *Mercury* asserted that it would have no effect on the black population, but its discussion of the matter revealed its apprehension.[33] The other fear was that it would interfere with foreign recognition of the Confederacy. "No harm will be done in Europe," the Arkansas *State Gazette* claimed, "for recognition will come only when the last hope is gone of being crushed by the abolitionists."[34] A Charleston editor was certain that the prevention of the recognition of the Confederacy by England was one of the principal reasons for the Proclamation. He admitted that it would doubtless gratify the feelings of a large portion of the "ignorant and misguided British public," and this seemed to depress him.

While the Proclamation elicited immediate reaction all over the world, it was not nearly so overwhelmingly favorable to the Union as the Confederates feared or as the North hoped. A circular containing the text of the Proclamation was sent out by the Department of State to all diplomatic and consular officers in foreign countries on September 24, 1862. Even before governments indicated their reactions, the foreign press had begun to comment on the Proclamation. In Canada the Toronto *Globe* regarded the Proclamation right as well as politic, and stated that it would be sustained by the voice of the civilized world.[35] "A large portion of the Slave States will be in rebellion on the 1st January next; and long ere that, we trust there will be an army of colored men on foot who will be able to fight for their own freedom."[36] One influential anti-Northern paper in Canada, the Napanee *Standard*, became more friendly to the North because it regarded the Proclamation as a "bold humanitarian act."[37] But the Toronto *Leader* entered a dissenting opinion, indicating that it was a war measure and would fail "to effect any good in that or any other respect."[38]

While the Preliminary Proclamation became the object of wide discussion abroad, the official and unofficial comments did little to encourage the Lincoln Administration. In Britain, the support for emancipation had always been strong among the working classes.[39] But the attitude of government officials and the business community, hardly encouraging to the Union, was summed up in the lines published in *Punch* early in the war:

> *Though with the North we sympathise,*
> *It must not be forgotten*
> *That with the South we've stronger ties,*
> *Which are composed of cotton,*
> *Whereof our imports mount unto*
> *A sum of many figures*
> *And where would be our calico*
> *Without the toil of niggers?*[40]

Two weeks after Lincoln issued the Preliminary Proclamation the British Chancellor of the Exchequer, William Gladstone, made his famous speech in Newcastle in which he declared that the Confederacy had, indeed, made a nation. "We may anticipate with certainty the success of the Southern States sofar as regards their separation from the North."[41] About the same time, commenting on the President's Proclamation, Lord Palmerston, the Prime Minister, called it a "singular manifesto that could scarcely be treated seriously. It is not easy to estimate how utterly powerless and contemptible a government must have become which could sanction with its approval such . . . trash."[42]

Henry Sanford, the United States Minister to Belgium, visited London in early October 1862 and concluded that since the "masses are of little account and the middling classes more looked to," the United States had made no gain by the Emancipation Proclamation.[43] Perhaps it was this distressing state of affairs that caused Charles Francis Adams, the United States Minister to Great Britain, to report to his government on October 10 that the effect of the Proclamation "has been generally to strengthen feeling on both sides."[44]

Meanwhile Lord Lyons, the British Minister to the United States, received word from London that the Proclamation was being unfavorably received in England. It is a "brutum fulmen," one correspondent told him. "It is merely a Confiscation Act, or perhaps worse, for it offers direct encouragement to servile insurrections." Lord Russell, the British Foreign Secretary, commented that, as a result of the Proclamation, "a premium will be given to acts of plunder, of incendiarism, and of revenge." Obviously the military and naval authorities of the United States would be bound to maintain and protect the perpetrators of such acts.[45]

Adams was doubtless even more depressed by the reaction of the British Press. The influential Manchester *Guardian* said on October 7 that the Proclamation had been "too hastily regarded as announcing an approaching abolition of slavery throughout the United States." As a matter of fact, the editor contended, it did no more than repeat the three alternatives outlined by Lincoln in his famous letter to Greeley in August. "It could lead to any of the three. . . . It is evidently nothing more than a compound of 'bunkum' on a grand scale with the swaggering bravado so conspicuous throughout the present war."

While the *Guardian* had little sympathy for the Palmerston-Gladstone position, it could not see anything praiseworthy in the Proclamation. A week later the editor declared that the federal politicians could not be given the slightest credit for any regard for humanity and freedom, "seeing that the privilege of holding fellow creatures in bondage, which is to be penally abolished in the contumacious states is to be reserved with fresh assurances and guarantees, as a reward for the obsequious fidelity of those which consent to adhere to the Union."[46]

The *Spectator* was not disposed to exult over the President's manifesto. "It is only a hopeful promise" that completely disregards the basic principle at stake. "The principle asserted is not that a human being cannot justly own another, but that he cannot own him unless he is loyal to the United States." Perhaps such a position could satisfy Americans, but it could hardly be expected to elicit enthusiasm from the outside world. "The South should be fought with an idea—it has one—only this way can the North really prosecute the war and enlist enthusiasm."[47]

The *Times* was the most influential paper in London, and Henry Sanford was painfully correct when he said that "its Dicta . . . seems to be gospel to the Commoners." This would seem to spell doom to the Union cause in Britain, for the *Times* was unusually hostile to the Proclamation. It would be of no effect, the editor frankly stated on October 6, but it would "force continuation of the war by the South to its last extremity." On the following day the *Times* accused Lincoln of seeking to excite a servile war. "He will appeal to the black blood of the African; he will whisper of the pleasures of spoil and of the gratification of yet fiercer instincts; and when blood begins to flow and shrieks come piercing through the darkness, Mr. Lincoln will wait till the rising flames tell that all is consummated, and then he will rub his hands and think that revenge is sweet."[48] Few Confederate editors exceeded the London *Times* in its denunciation of the Proclamation as an atrocious measure, hardly worthy of a civilized nation.

The *Economist* declared that the justice of the *Times* attack on the Proclamation could not be maintained. Lincoln's measure was indeed dishonest and foolish, but not atrocious. "If it were aimed at servile war or likely to cause such it would be atrocious." But blacks could be expected to do no more than not work and, as a result, white manpower would have to be diverted from the front. The worst thing about the Proclamation was that if the slave-holders were overcome by Union forces by the end of December, the promised freedom to the slaves would vanish.[49] The *Saturday Review* voiced a similar view. The Proclamation was a "lawless stretch of arbitrary prerogative," and was all the more objectionable because it actually provided nothing for the blacks' future. "It presents the menace of murder and plunder. Conformity is to be rewarded by the perpetuation of slavery."[50]

The brightest light on the British horizon for the Union cause was the enthusiastic support given to the Proclamation by the laboring classes. In various parts of the country groups of workingmen celebrated the issuance of the Proclamation, and some of them voiced their approval in messages to Lincoln. A group of inhabitants of Birmingham expressed to him their strong belief in the justice of his cause, "of our warm sympathy with your noble effort for emancipation; and of our certain faith in your ultimate triumph."[51] Late in the year the workingmen of Manchester sent to the President an address in which they pledged him their support. They told him that if he had any ill-wishers in England, "be assured they are chiefly those who oppose liberty at home, and that they will be powerless to stir up quarrels between us. . . . Accept our high admiration of your firmness in upholding the proclamation of freedom."[52] In the fall of 1862 Charles Francis Adams had something good to report to his government in Washington.

The most favorable reaction in the British press was the view expressed by the London *Star* that praised the Union's policy of prospective compensation and confiscation. "Is this not a gigantic stride in the paths of Christian and civilized progress? Is not here a reason, abundant and unquestionable, why every man to whom personal or political freedom is dear should pray for the success of the Union arms?"[53] The views of the *Star* and British workingmen and the diligent efforts of Minister Charles Francis Adams did much to hold the tide against official Britain until events of an economic and military nature could fasten Britain to a more unequivocal neutrality than it was inclined to pursue in the fall of 1862.

French reaction was not unlike that of the British. The week after the issuance of the Proclamation, France's Minister to the United States, Henri Mercier, told his government that it was mainly to disarm European interference. He predicted that this move by the Union would lead to anarchy, horrible carnage, and crimes too revolting to mention. "On the basis, I question if the moment has not arrived for the governments of Europe to make a serious effort to prevent the events from which they would have to suffer so cruelly themselves."[54]

While the French government did not take Mercier's suggestion seriously, the reaction of the government and much of the press was generally no less critical. William L. Dayton, the United States Minister to France, predicted that the press would "pervert and misconstrue" the motives that prompted the Proclamation and the probable consequences that will follow it." On October 21 he handed M. Drouyn de Lhuys, the French Foreign Minister, a copy of the Proclamation. Dayton received the distinct impression on this and later occasions that the French government and the semiofficial press were more anxious for a "cessation of hostilities before the next cotton crop was harvested than in emancipation."[55]

The French press seemed to bear out Dayton's views of French reaction. *Le Constitutionnel* called it a war measure "that does not do honor to the moral sense of its signer or the government that approved it."[56] *La France* found the Proclamation not convincing. "It looks no higher than a general butchery of defenseless women and children."[57] *Presse* found it "unsatisfactory," for as a half-measure it satisfied no one.[58]

The President's measure had its French supporters, however; a correspondent of the New York *Times* reported that the liberal press and the general public unanimously approved the Proclamation.[59] This was a bit excessive and did not jibe with the report of Henry Sanford, who was visiting Paris at the end of October. He was of the opinion that public opinion was all wrong in Paris and the Proclamation had been used, with effect, against the United States. He reported that Prince Murat, the liberal member of the Bonaparte family, told him that the United States was carrying on war in a manner that shocked Frenchmen. "It is not only wanting in the chivalrique character of our conduct of war but it is unhuman and barbarian. . . ."[60] But the *Journal des Débats* declared that the Proclamation would strike an irreparable blow at the peculiar institution, "time and the contagion of liberty will do the rest."[61] *Patrie* thought the President was right in saying to the Confederates, "you who refuse to come to us we will follow with our hate, with pillage and ruin."[62]

These mixed reactions made it difficult for Dayton or anyone else to evaluate properly the French reaction to the Proclamation. It doubtless had the desired effect, however; for at no time after its issuance did the French government give serious consideration to the possibility of active intervention on the side of the Confederacy.

In other parts of western Europe the reaction seemed more favorable. At his post in Brussels, Henry Sanford read the circular to M. Rojier, the Belgian Foreign Minister, on October 7. Rojier expressed the fear that the Proclamation would tend to prolong and add exasperation to the war, but he expressed no hostility to it.[63] Horatio J. Perry, the United States Minister to Spain, presented the Proclamation to officials of the Spanish government on October 23. Neither Calderon Gollantes, nor the Duke of Tetuan, both prominent in the Spanish government, made any unfavorable comment about the document. They did, however, express some apprehension about the ultimate effect of the Proclamation on slavery in Cuba. "But the Proclamation has struck the popular heart of Spain," Perry reported. "The cause of the Government of Washington has gained strength in Spain and will continue to gain immensely as the full import of this proclamation comes to be popularly recognized and appreciated."[64]

Gustavus Koener, en route to Madrid to replace Perry, visited several European countries in early October before taking up his new duties. He found very little sympathy in France, "though no hostility amongst the people." In Germany and Switzerland, Koener found almost everyone friendly to the Union. He was more certain than some of his colleagues that the Proclamation would generally enhance the prestige of the United States in Europe.[65]

Russia's reservations regarding the Proclamation grew, in part, out of the feeling that it was not nearly so significant and far-reaching as its own emancipation of the serfs the previous year. In part it grew out of the critical reports of Baron de Stoeckl, the Russian Minister to the United States. It was a "futile menace," he said, forced upon Lincoln by the radicals in a desperate effort to maintain their waning powers. In a lengthy dispatch on September 25 devoted primarily to military developments Stoeckl told his government that the Proclamation settled the question "only halfway." It was used by the President "as a military weapon to subdue his enemies and is not at all a proclamation of human liberty."[66] The semiofficial *Journal of St. Petersburg*, however, gave indication of support of the Proclamation. It had been silent during the Union reverses earlier in the year; but after the publication of the Proclamation, it carried much more pro-Union material.[67]

Reaction in Russia was, indeed, mixed. While there was some genuine sympathy with the North, there was much greater interest in the war's coming to a speedy conclusion. Thus, Stoeckl was unhappy about the Proclamation largely because he feared that it decreased the chances for an early end to the war. Fëdor Dostoevski is said to have been depressed by Lincoln's decree because he was certain that it would lead to "unheard-of savagery" and a prolongation of the war.[68] Likewise, the Russian Foreign Minister, Prince Gorchakov, was greatly relieved to learn that the war had not become a crusade against slavery and that the Proclamation would be dropped if the South would simply acknowledge federal authority and reunite on the basis of the Constitution.[69]

The initial European reaction to the Proclamation could give the government in Washington little comfort. Some Europeans were sympathetic to the Confederacy and reacted unfavorably to this latest gambit by Lincoln. Others, more neutral, doubted that it could have any significant effect or had grave doubts about the legality of the move. Even many who were deeply committed to the Union cause were disappointed because it was "coldly indifferent" to the moral and humanitarian aspects of slavery. The number of articulate Europeans who were enthusiastic about the Proclamation seemed pitifully small. Only gradually, as Union victories gave support to the Proclamation, did its effect on European attitudes become clear.

The Proclamation was not to go into effect until January 1, 1863. And until that date there was no way of knowing what states or portions of states would be back in the Union and thus escape the effects of the Proclamation. Yet, it is significant that the Washington government took great pains to indicate to the military commanders that the Preliminary Proclamation had been issued. After all, it was a military measure; and, under the circumstances, the distribution of 15,000 copies among the military did not seem excessive. These copies were dispatched to the various commanders in the field on September 24, 1862, as General Orders 139.[70] No special instruction accompanied the Orders, but it was expected that the information would be passed on among the army's rank and file.

Some commanding officers appreciated the full significance of the Proclamation and hoped that it would fire their men to a more vigorous pursuit of the enemy. Some were so completely out of sympathy with the emancipation policy that they resigned their commissions and went home.[71] Some, like General George B. McClellan, then in command of the Army of the Potomac, sought to keep dissatisfaction and misunderstanding at a minimum by discouraging discussion of the measure. On October 7, 1862, McClellan issued an order in which he warned his men that discussion of "public measures determined upon and declared by the Government, when carried at all beyond temperate and respectful opinion, tend to impair and destroy discipline and efficiency" among the troops.[72] McClellan might have discouraged public discussion on the part of his men, but one doubts that he or any other officer could have prevented discussion and even heated debate in the privacy of the barracks.

Within a matter of days after the Preliminary Proclamation was issued its contents were known to most of the Union soldiers. Some were opposed to making the war for the Union a "Negro War," and they bitterly denounced Lincoln. One newspaper reporter observed that many soldiers were unhappy about the Proclamation. "Slavery is already practically abolished but the Proclamation is a different affair, and if it should not be received more kindly by other Officers of the Army than those whom I have seen it will go far towards producing an expression on the part of the Army that will startle the Country and give us a military Dictator."[73] But there were other soldiers who were greatly encouraged, taking the view that the cause of freedom must be paramount. Perhaps most soldiers were not clear on why they were fighting or what they wanted except to defeat those who seemed determined to destroy their country.

If anything, the Confederate soldiers reacted much more vigorously to the Proclamation than did the Union troops. The new Lincoln policy clearly sought to undermine Southern institutions, and neither the Southern press nor the Confederate officers permitted the rank and file of the Confederate Army to forget it for a moment. General Simon Bolivar Buckner, speaking in Kentucky two days after the Proclamation was issued, told prospective Confederate soldiers that their only disloyalty was to "the tyranny and usurpation, which seek to take from you even the right of peaceful remonstrance." He called on the people of Kentucky to join the Confederacy in the task of extinguishing "the servile torch" by which the Union intended to destroy their homes and their civilization."[74] Surely Confederate soldiers now knew the war aims of the Union. And knowing them, their own aims became much clearer to them.

One of Lincoln's hopes, in issuing the Preliminary Proclamation, was to deprive the South of its slave labor force, thus undermining the military effectiveness of the Confederacy. He and Stanton knew that the word of emancipation would get through to the slaves, and they hoped that many would leave their masters. They must have known, too, that the South would double its efforts to keep the slaves under control. The Governor of South Carolina said in November 1862 that the Proclamation would produce none of the effects intended by its "vulgar author," but he advised the legislature to strengthen the state guard in the event that any deluded blacks attempted a servile insurrection. In many communities citizens pledged to maintain greater control than ever over their slaves by keeping them at home and forbidding them to leave the plantation without passes.

Even before the issuance of the Preliminary Proclamation slaveholders experienced real difficulty in keeping their slaves under control. For more than a year thousands of slaves had been coming into the Union lines, and the Union commanders had long since concluded that they should not be returned to their masters. In Virginia, Tennessee, Louisiana, wherever the Union armies went, slaves joined them much to the distress and consternation of their former owners. After the Confiscation Act was passed in July 1862, colonies of contrabands were organized, and many of them were employed to assist the Union cause. Contraband and freedmen relief associations were organized in Northern cities. Slave desertion of the plantation was a major problem in the Confederacy before Lincoln's Proclamation was issued.[75]

Before the end of September, blacks began to learn of the Proclamation. The Southern press printed the document, and the slaves who could read shared it with others. Isaac Lane, later a bishop in the Colored Methodist Church, took from his master's mailbox the newspaper containing the Proclamation and read it to other slaves. Whites were so filled with consternation that they discussed the Proclamation without bothering to notice if slaves themselves were listening. Frequently they were, and they passed the word along. The Proclamation was so widely known among the slaves before the end of September that the New York *Times* was moved to remark "that there is far more rapid and secret diffusing of intelligence and news throughout the plantations than was ever dreamed of in the North."[76]

If Lincoln made a clear distinction in his Proclamation between loyal and rebel states, the slaves themselves did not follow his reasoning. In the same way that slaves in rebel states did not wait until January 1 to see if they were free, slaves in border states seemed to ignore the fact that the Proclamation would not apply to them in any case. In Maryland they began to act as freedmen, and many went into the nation's capital to live. In Kentucky there were so many asserting their freedom that the Louisville *Journal* asked black leaders to explain to slaves that the Proclamation did not affect slavery in Kentucky.[77] Whether he was in the heart of the Confederacy or in the border city of Baltimore, the black slave after September 22 knew that something wonderful was in the offing for him. And his movements, his restiveness, and his new enthusiasm for the Union cause indicated that he knew what it was.

The issuance of the Emancipation Proclamation added one more complicating factor to the confused political picture as the nation prepared for the fall elections in 1862. The Lincoln Administration was already the target of vehement critics who seized every opportunity to attempt to persuade the voters that the government in Washington was unworthy of their confidence. And there were numerous opportunities. Military reverses, rising prices and taxes, the suspension of the writ of habeas corpus, and generally the heavy hand of wartime government policies were among the more obvious conditions that Lincoln's critics exploited. If the Proclamation transformed the war into a crusade against slavery, thousands of ardent supporters of the Union would no longer be interested; and confidence in Lincoln, who had declared that the preservation of the Union was the paramount issue, would be undermined.

As early as July the Postmaster General, Montgomery Blair, who fancied himself the political specialist in the Cabinet, had predicted that a proclamation to free the slaves would cost the Republicans the fall elections. In view of numerous other areas of difficulty for the Republicans this could hardly be accurate. But Lincoln was too astute a politician to ignore the possible effect of the Proclamation on Republican chances. In the weeks that followed the announcement of his emancipation policy he was depressed by the loud critics who predicted ruin for the Republicans. The war Democrats insisted that he had betrayed the original aims of the war. The radical Republicans condemned him for the conservative course he was pursuing. There seemed to be little that the President could do at this juncture except to concentrate on the conduct of the war with the hope that a favorable turn of the tide would be reflected in Republican victories at the polls.

In New York the Democrats were especially vigorous in their attack on the Proclamation. It was a proposal "for the butchery of women and children, for scenes of lust and rapine, and of arson and murder. . . ."[78] But the lack of military successes caused more disaffection in New York than the Emancipation Proclamation.[79] In Massachusetts Governor Andrew embraced the Proclamation as a "mighty act" and urged voters to elect Republicans who would help the President achieve freedom and victory.[80] That is what they proceeded to do.

In the West the situation was far from bright for the Republicans. H. S. Bundy, a Union candidate for Congress in Ohio said in early October that the Proclamation had come "just in the nick of time to save the country, perhaps, while from present appearances it will defeat me and every other Union candidate for Congress along the border."[81] During the campaign Democrats excited the voters by predicting the mass migration into Ohio of emancipated blacks. Former Senator William Allen emerged from retirement to declare that "Every white laboring man in the North who does not want to be swapped off for a free nigger should vote the Democratic ticket."[82] Many of them apparently followed his advice.

The story was essentially the same in some other Western states. Republicans in Indiana greatly feared that the Proclamation would cause them to lose the state. Some conservative Union papers printed the Proclamation without comment, while others angrily denounced it and announced their support of the Democrats. Republican leader Oliver P. Morton ignored the larger implications of the Proclamation and called it a "stratagem of War," but Hoosiers were not pleased. They registered their objection at the polls.[83] In Illinois, Democratic newspapers called for a repudiation of the President because the Proclamation would prolong the war.[84] Small wonder that John Hay, visiting in Illinois late in October, wrote his White House colleague, John G. Nicolay, "Things look badly around here politically."[85] They looked even worse after the election.

It was in Michigan that the Republicans gave the Administration its strongest support in the West. The battle of Antietam and the Proclamation were hailed with joy by the Union supporters, who heard their leader, Zachariah Chandler, put the best possible interpretation on both events. Meanwhile, the governor, Austin Blair, called on all loyal citizens to endorse the President's stand.[86] They tolerated no indifference or criticism; and they succeeded in achieving victory over the Democrats.

The elections did not bring much in the way of good news to Lincoln. In October the Democrats carried Pennsylvania, Ohio, and Indiana. In the following month they were successful in New York, New Jersey, Illinois, and Delaware. In New England, Kansas, Missouri, Michigan, Iowa, and California, Republican victories ranged from moderate to decisive. It was a serious Administration set-back, but not as disastrous as some Democrats claimed.[87]

Lincoln ascribed the Republican reverses to the involve-ment of leading Republicans in the war effort, the frenzied efforts of Democrats to take advantage of this situation, and the lack of military successes.[88] Undoubtedly the Proclama-tion gained votes for the Administration in some places such as New England, Michigan, and Kansas. But adverse reactions to it in Indiana, Pennsylvania, and elsewhere hurt the Administration. It was one factor among many that sent the Republicans down to defeat. There hardly seemed jus-tification, however, for the observation of Karl Marx who said in mid-November, "Of Lincoln's emancipation . . . one still sees no effect up to the present, save that from fear of a Negro inundation the Northwest has voted Democratic."[89]

Some critics of the Administration and opponents of the Proclamation hoped that the Republican losses in the elec-tion might deter Lincoln from issuing the Proclamation on January 1. He was visibly shaken by the reverses at the polls in October and November. Everyone waited to see if these defeats would cause him to modify his announced policy regarding freedom for the slaves.

In his second annual message, which he sent to Con-gress on December 1, 1862, the President gave little indica-tion that he had changed his mind, but his emphasis was different. He seemed as determined as ever to colonize blacks in some other part of the world, but he had not been successful. In referring to the Proclamation of September 22, the President passed quickly to the subject of compen-sated emancipation. He hoped that Congress would adopt a resolution to amend the Constitution providing for com-pensated emancipation. This would shorten the war, insure an increase of population, and promote national prosperity. He urged this plan as a way of restoring the union and making unnecessary the issuance of the final Proclamation.[90]

While the President did not threaten Congress, the inference could easily be drawn that if Congress did not adopt some plan for compensated emancipation, he would proceed to issue the final Proclamation at the appointed time. Congress had one month in which to act, and it began immediately to discuss the problem. Lincoln's critics had no interest in complying with his request, however. Instead, they proceeded to heap criticisms and threats on the President. On December 5, for example, the fiercely critical Clement L. Vallandigham of Ohio offered a resolution declaring that "anyone attempting to turn the war into one that would overthrow the institutions of the States shall be guilty of a high crime." It did not pass. A few days later Representative Hendrick B. Wright of Pennsylvania asked the House to declare that the war was "inaugurated *solely* for the suppression of the rebellion and the restoration of the Union as it was. . . ." Any attempts to change this policy should be regarded as "a fraud upon the gallant men" living and dead who have fought to save their country. On the same day, December 8, William A. Richardson of Illinois asserted that the Proclamation was unconstitutional. He said that it had driven into the army of the South every person it was possible to drive there.

By the middle of December the discussion in Congress was moving into its final stage. John W. Menzies of Kentucky said the abolitionist program was responsible for the Republican defeat in the fall elections and although he had never been a Democrat he rejoiced in their victory. The people have condemned the Proclamation, said Samuel S. Cox of Ohio, yet "we have the presidential message, which proposes to adhere to the condemned proclamation." George Yeaman of Kentucky said that even the President himself realized that the Proclamation was unconstitutional, and he had indicated as much when he overruled Frémont and Hunter. This emancipation measure, said James A. Cravens of Indiana, seems to contemplate the bursting up of the old relations of society that have long existed in the Southern states. "The people would never consent to it, and it was not an issue at the beginning of the war."

John W. Crisfield of Maryland made an impassioned speech in which he said that the President had yielded to racial elements. "Manfully had he struggled, and firmly had he stood, when the danger seemed greatest. . . . As the thunderbolt from a cloudless sky, the *proclamation*, fell upon the country, men stood mute in amazement. Its suddenness, its utter contempt for the Constitution, its imperial pretension, the thorough upheaving of the whole social organization which it decreed, and the perspective of crime, and blood, and ruin, which it opened to the vision, filled every patriotic heart with astonishment, terror and indignation."

The President had some supporters in Congress, but they were neither as vehement nor as vocal as his enemies. John Hutchins of Ohio praised the Proclamation as a proper exercise of war powers to undercut the labor force of the South. John W. Noell of Missouri said that slavery had become an element of national destruction and it therefore ought to die. William D. Kelley of Pennsylvania said that the enemies who attempted to overthrow the government, "lose their title to constitutional rights, and it becomes the duty of the government, by whatever force it may require, to regain possession and control of the territory occupied by them."

Perhaps the greatest comfort to Lincoln came from the passage by a vote of 78–51 of a resolution sponsored by Samuel C. Fessenden of Maine approving the issuance of the Emancipation Proclamation. The resolution said that the Proclamation was "warranted by the Constitution; that the policy of emancipation, as indicated in the proclamation is well adapted to hasten the restoration of peace, was well chosen as a war measure, and is an exercise of power, with

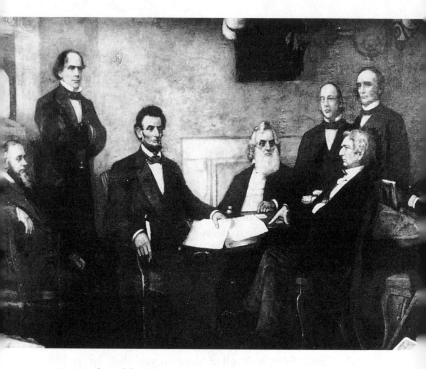

First Reading of the Emancipation Proclamation, July 22, 1862. This celebrated painting by Francis B. Carpenter was presented to Congress in 1878. The members of the Cabinet are, left to right, Edwin M. Stanton, Secretary of War; Salmon P. Chase, Secretary of the Treasury; President Lincoln; Gideon Welles, Secretary of the Navy; Caleb B. Smith; Secretary of the Interior; William H. Seward, Secretary of State; Montgomery Blair, Postmaster General; and Edward Bates, Attorney General. *Courtesy, National Archives*

Opposite: The document Lincoln read to his cabinet on July 22, 1862.

In pursuance of the sixth section of the act of congress entitled "An act to suppress insurrection and to punish treason and rebellion, to seize and confiscate property of rebels, and for other purposes" Approved July 17. 1862, and which act, and the joint Resolution explanatory thereof, are herewith published, I, Abraham Lincoln, President of the United States, do hereby proclaim to, and warn all persons within the contemplation of said sixth section to cease participating in, aiding, countenancing, or abetting the existing rebellion, or any rebellion against the government of the United States, and to return to their proper allegiance to the United States, on pain of the forfeitures and seizures, as within and by said sixth section provided—

And I hereby make known that it is my purpose, upon the next meeting of Congress, to again recommend the adoption of a practical measure for tendering pecuniary aid to the free choice or rejection, of any and all States which may then be recognizing and practically sustaining the authority of the United States, and which may then have voluntarily adopted, or thereafter may voluntarily adopt, gradual abolishment of slavery within such State or States—that the object is to practically restore, thenceforward to maintain, the constitutional relation between the general government, and each, and all the states, wherein that relation is now suspended, or disturbed; and that, for this object, the war, as it has been, will be, prosecuted. And, as a fit and necessary military measure for effecting this object, I, as Commander-in-Chief of the Army and

Navy of the United States, do order and declare that on the first day of January in the
year of our Lord one thousand eight hundred
and sixty-three, all persons held as slaves within any state or states, wherein the constitutional authority of the United States shall not
then be practically recognized, submitted to,
and maintained, shall then, thenceforward and
forever, be free.

From an etching by Dr. Adalbert J. Volck, a Baltimore dentist who was bitterly opposed to Lincoln and emancipation. On the wall is a portrait of John Brown, "St. Ossawotamie," and a picture alleging the violence and chaos that followed the abolition of slavery in St. Domingo. Lincoln has one foot on a copy of the Constitution and is using ink from the devil's inkpot with which to write the Proclamation.

Opposite, bottom: "Now if you don't come down, I'll cut the tree from under you." Sketched by a staff artist, this cartoon appeared in *Harper's Weekly*, October 11, 1862, and graphically depicts the sentiment expressed in the Preliminary Emancipation Proclamation of September 22, 1862.

This drawing by the well-known artist Thomas Nast appeared in *Harper's Weekly*, January 24, 1863. It is typical of the Nast sketches, which are known for their elaborate detail and their vigorous advocacy of a point of view.

All SLAVES were made FREEMEN

BY ABRAHAM LINCOLN,

PRESIDENT OF THE UNITED STATES,

JANUARY 1st, 1863.

Come, then, able-bodied COLORED MEN, to the nearest U. S. Camp, and fight for the

STARS AND STRIPES!

Top: This is one of several posters used by the Army to announce emancipation. Since President Lincoln announced in the Proclamation a policy of receiving blacks into the armed services, recruitment of black troops was frequently closely allied with the announcement. Bottom: Company E, 4th United States Colored Infantry at Fort Lincoln, Washington, D.C. *Courtesy, Library of Congress, NEG. # LC-B8171-7890*

After the battle of Antietam, September 17, 1862, President Lincoln visited the army of the Potomac. This photograph, taken on October 4, 1862, shows the President and "Little Mac" in McClellan's tent at headquarters. *Courtesy, Library of Congress, NEG. # LC-USZ62-2621.* Overleaf: The Preliminary Emancipation Proclamation of September 22, 1862.

By the President of the
United States of America
A Proclamation

I Abraham Lincoln, President of the United
States of America, and commander-in-chief
of the Army and Navy thereof, do hereby proclaim and declare that hereafter, as heretofore, the war will be prosecuted for the object of practically restoring the constitutional relation between the United States, and each
of the states, and the people thereof, in which
states that relation is, or may be suspended, or
disturbed.

That it is my purpose, upon the next meeting
of Congress to again recommend the adoption of
a practical measure tendering pecuniary aid to
the free acceptance or rejection of all slave
states, so called, the people whereof may not then
be in rebellion against the United States, and
which states, may then have voluntarily accepted, or thereafter may voluntarily adopt, immediate, or gradual abolishment of slavery within their respective limits; and that the effort
to colonize persons of African descent upon this
continent, or elsewhere, will be continued.

That on the first day of January in the year of
our Lord, one thousand eight hundred and sixty
three, all persons held as slaves within any
state, or designated part of a state, the people
whereof shall then be in rebellion against the
United States, shall be then, thenceforward,
and forever free; and the executive government of the United States, will, ~~during the con-~~
including the military and naval authority thereof
~~tinuance~~ ~~office of the present incumbent~~, recognize, such persons, ~~as being free~~, ~~and~~ ~~will~~
and maintain the freedom of
do no act or acts to repress such persons or any
of them in any efforts they may make for their
actual freedom.

That the executive will, on the first day of Jan-
nary aforesaid, by proclamation, designate the
States, and parts of states, if any, in which the
people thereof respectively, shall then be in rebellion against the United States; and the fact
that any state, or the people thereof shall, on
that day be, in good faith represented in the
Congress of the United States, by members chosen
thereto at elections wherein a majority of the

qualified voters of such state shall have participated, shall, in the absence of strong countervailing testimony, be deemed conclusive evidence that such state and the people thereof, are not then in rebellion against the United States.

That attention is hereby called to an Act of Congress entitled "An act to make an additional Article of War" approved March 13. 1862, and which act is in the words and figure following:

Also to the. ninth. and tenth sections of an Act entitled "An Act to suppress Insurrection; to punish Treason and Rebellion, to seize and confiscate property of rebels, and for other purposes," approved July 17. 1862, and which sections are in the words and figures following:

And I do hereby enjoin upon and order all persons engaged in the military and naval service of the United States to observe, obey, and enforce, within their respective spheres of service, the acts, and sections above recited.

And the executive will in due time recommend that all citizens of the United States who shall have remained loyal thereto throughout the rebellion, shall (upon the restoration of the constitutional relation between the United States, and their respective states, and people, if that relation shall have been suspended or disturbed) be compensation for all losses by acts of the United States, including the loss of slaves.

In witness whereof, I have hereunto set my hand, and caused the seal of the United States to be affixed.

L. S.

Done at the City of Washington, this twenty second day of September, in the year of our Lord, one thousand, eight hundred and sixty two, and of the Independence of the United States, the eighty seventh.

Abraham Lincoln.

By the President:
William H. Seward,
Secretary of State

proper regard for the rights of the States, and the prosperity of free Government."[91] As long as it was clear that the majority of the members stood by him, the blatant cries of the minority were not quite so distressing to Lincoln.

There were others who sought to influence the President's actions as the Hundred Days came to a close. In late November a delegation of ardent Unionists from Kentucky called on him and urged him to issue the Proclamation, as he had promised to do. He told his visitors that he would "rather die than take back a word of the Proclamation of Freedom. . . ."[92] In early December, Charles Kirkland, a New York lawyer, sent to the President a copy of his reply to Benjamin Curtis' published attack on the Proclamation.[93] In his pamphlet Kirkland reviewed the constitutional and legal basis for the Proclamation and concluded that the President had ample authority to issue the Proclamation. He urged him to do so.[94] In acknowledging his receipt of the pamphlet Lincoln told Kirkland, "It appears to me to be a paper of great ability, and for the country's sake, more than my own, I thank you for it."[95]

Henry J. Raymond, the editor of the influential New York *Times*, gave support to the President as he presumably prepared the final draft of the Proclamation. He told the President that he hoped that he would not attempt to make the war subservient to the sweeping abolition of slavery, for that would drive the border states from the Union and divide the country. The use of emancipation as a military weapon, however, would gain the support of the entire loyal country, including the border states. "I suggest, then, that the Proclamation to be issued in January, *take the form of a* MILITARY ORDER. . . ." The President thanked Raymond and said that he would remember and consider his suggestions.[96]

As the end of the year approached, Lincoln's difficulties multiplied. At Fredericksburg, Virginia, in mid-December, Burnside's army had been crushed by the Confederates. On the heels of this disaster, the pressures increased on the President to reorganize his Administration. Some wanted him to get rid of Seward. Others wanted Chase to go. Both submitted resignations, which the President did not accept. Only after spending days in the effort to clear the air of rumors and false accusations was the President able to establish the point that the Cabinet was his *own* official family and that he alone would make the decisions regarding its reorganization. This took valuable time away from the prosecution of the War and the drafting of the final draft of the Emancipation Proclamation.[97]

The reverses at Fredericksburg and the Cabinet crisis created a situation not unlike that which caused the President to reach a decision on emancipation in June. Things were again going "from bad to worse," and something needed to be done. This time the thing to be done was to issue the final Proclamation. Sumner visited the President on Christmas Eve, and the two men discussed at length the Emancipation Proclamation. Lincoln told Sumner that he would not stop the Proclamation if he could, and he could not if he would.[98] Sumner said "Hallelujah," but there were others who were not so pleased. The President was fatally bent upon his course, complained Senator Orville H. Browning of Illinois, "saying that if he should refuse to issue his proclamation there would be a rebellion in the north, and that a dictator would be placed over his head within a week. There is no hope. The Proclamation will come—God grant it may not be productive of the mischief I fear."[99]

Washington had a quiet Christmas. Congress was in recess from December 24 until January 5, and many members went to their respective homes. For some, this was a relief from the "noisy and loud professions" that filled the Houses for the better part of a month. The Cabinet remained, and it met almost daily during the last week in December. On the day after Christmas, there was a lengthy discussion of the matter of making a new state of West Virginia, and the President asked all members of the Cabinet to file their opinions with him. This was an important matter; but while it was concerned with a portion of only one of the seceded states another urgent matter, emancipation, concerned all of them.

At the meeting of the Cabinet on December 29, Lincoln read a draft of his Emancipation Proclamation, invited criticism, and directed that copies be provided for each member of the Cabinet. The only substantive suggestion, made by Chase, was that fractional parts of states ought not to be exempted. Welles agreed, observing that "there would be difficulty in freeing parts of States and not freeing others,— a clashing between central and local authorities."[100]

On December 30, at the Cabinet meeting, copies of the Proclamation were distributed to members of the Cabinet. There ensued a lively discussion in which several members, notably Edward Bates, the Attorney General, offered suggestions. Bates thought that the executive branch should use the military and naval forces to maintain the freedom of the former slaves. He also suggested that the President call on blacks to "show themselves worthy of freedom by fidelity and diligence in the employments which may be given to them by the observance of order and by abstaining from all violence not required by duty or for self defence."[101] The suggestions of Seward and Blair were largely of an editorial nature.

On Wednesday morning, December 31, at ten o'clock, the Cabinet held its final meeting of the year. When the Proclamation was taken up, Seward and Welles suggested an amendment "enjoining upon, instead of appealing to, those emancipated, to forbear from tumult."[102] Chase submitted a lengthy communication, making suggestions of changes and offering his own draft of the Proclamation. He repeated his objection to exemption of "parts of States from the operation of the Proclamation. . . ." He also thought that the Proclamation should omit the statement that the government would not act to repress those newly emancipated in any efforts they may make for their actual freedom. He reminded the President that this statement in the September Proclamation was widely quoted as an incitement to servile insurrection. Likewise he objected to any reference to the military employment of the former slaves, "leaving it to the natural course of things already well begun."

Chase then submitted his own draft embodying the views he had expressed and containing the following felicitous closing, most of which Lincoln incorporated in his own draft:

> *And upon this act, sincerely believed to be an act of justice warranted by the constitution, [and an act of duty demanded by the circumstances of the country,]ᵃ I invoke the considerate judgment of mankind and the gracious favor of almighty God.*[103]

At long last Chase seemed to be having some influence. The President took the suggestions, "written in order, and said he would complete the document."

For the President the day was not over. There was the final draft of the Proclamation to prepare. There was the act to sign admitting West Virginia into the Union. There was the agreement to sign providing for a colony of freedmen on Ile a Vache. There was the delegation of antislavery leaders to listen to, with their plea that he issue the Proclamation as a simple act of justice rather than as a military measure. His "day" went far into the night.

By nightfall, blacks all over the country nervously awaited their "Day of Days." In Washington, close to the center of history, they crowded into the chapel in the contraband camp at Twelfth and Q Streets for the "watch night" meeting. There were prayers of thanksgiving and hallelujah hymns. One man rejoiced that wives and children could not be sold any more. It was near the break of day before they disbanded.[104]

In New York's Shiloh Presbyterian Church, there was a New Year's Eve Grand Emancipation Jubilee. Presiding at

---

ᵃ Lincoln omitted the phrase in brackets and in its place inserted, "upon military necessity."

the meeting was the church's pastor, the Reverend Henry Highland Garnet, who for years had been one of the country's outstanding black abolitionists. By nine o'clock the church was filled to overflowing, one third of the audience being white. Black and white speakers hailed the forthcoming proclamation as one of the great landmarks of human freedom. Reverend Simeon S. Jocelyn said that the most loyal people in the United States were the blacks. If the President had issued the Emancipation Proclamation at the beginning of the war, "the nation would have been saved the deluge of blood that had since flowed throughout the land." At 11:55 P.M. there was a five-minute period of silent prayer. At midnight the choir sang, "Blow Ye Trumpets Blow, the Year of Jubilee has come."[105]

Wherever blacks were on New Year's Eve, 1862, there was little time for sleeping!

4 Day of Days

Thursday, January 1, 1863, was a bright, crisp day in the nation's capital. The previous day had been a strenuous one for the President, but New Year's Day was to be even more strenuous. So he rose early. There was much to do, not the least of which was to put the finishing touches on the Proclamation. Before he could begin, the troubled General Ambrose E. Burnside, who had led the ill-fated Fredericksburg campaign, called at the White House. He was fully aware of the fact that he had lost the confidence of his men, and he told the President so. He felt, therefore, that he should retire to private life. The President calmed the general, who then returned to his men. Lincoln then proceeded to work on the Proclamation. When he had finished the draft he sent it over to the Department of State for the superscription and closing.

At 10:45 the document was brought to the White House by Secretary of State Seward. The President signed it, but he noticed an error in the superscription. It read, "In testimony whereof I have hereunto set my name and caused the seal of the United States to be affixed." The President had never used that form in proclamations, always preferring to say "In testimony whereof I have hereunto set my hand...." He asked Seward to make the correction; and the formal signing would be made on the corrected copy.[1]

The traditional New Year's Day reception at the White House began that morning at eleven o'clock. Members of the Cabinet and the diplomatic corps were among the first to arrive. Officers of the Army and Navy arrived in a body at half-past eleven. The public was admitted at noon, and the reception lasted until two o'clock. During the reception Seward and his son Frederick, the Assistant Secretary of State, returned with the corrected draft. The rigid laws of etiquette held the President to his duty for three hours, his secretaries, Nicolay and Hay, declared. "Had actual necessity required it, he could of course have left such mere social occupation at any moment; but the President saw no occasion for precipitancy. On the other hand, he probably deemed it wise that the completion of this momentous executive act should be attended by every circumstance of deliberation."[2]

After the guests departed the President went upstairs to his study for the signing in the presence of a few friends. No Cabinet meeting was called and no attempt was made to have a ceremony. Later, Lincoln told F. B. Carpenter the artist that as he took up the pen to sign the paper his hand shook so violently that he could not write. "I could not for a moment control my arm. I paused, and a superstitious feeling came over me which made me hesitate. . . . In a moment I remembered that I had been shaking hands for hours with several hundred people, and hence a very simple explanation of the trembling and shaking of my arm." With a hearty laugh at his own thoughts, the President proceeded to sign the Proclamation.[3] Just before he affixed his name to the document, he said, "I never, in my life, felt more certain that I was doing right than I do in signing this paper."

January 1, 1863*
BY THE PRESIDENT OF THE UNITED STATES OF AMERICA:
A Proclamation
Whereas, on the twentysecond day of September, in the year of our Lord one thousand eight hundred and sixty two, a proclamation was issued by the President of the

United States, containing, among other things, the following towit:

"That on the first day of January, in the year of our Lord one thousand eight hundred and sixty-three, all persons held as slaves within any State or designated part of a State, the people whereof shall then be in rebellion against the United States, shall be then, thenceforward, and forever free; and the Executive Government of the United States, including the military and naval authority thereof, will recognize and maintain the freedom of such persons, and will do no act or acts to repress such persons, or any of them, in any efforts they may make for their actual freedom.

"That the Executive will, on the first day of January aforesaid, by proclamation, designate the States and parts of States, if any, in which the people thereof, shall on that day be, in good faith, represented in the Congress of the United States by members chosen thereto at elections wherein a majority of the qualified voters of such State shall have participated, shall in the absence of strong countervailing testimony, be deemed conclusive evidence that such State, and the people thereof, are not then in rebellion against the United States."

Now, therefore, I, Abraham Lincoln, President of the United States, by virtue of the power in me invested as Commander-in-Chief, of the Army and Navy of the United States in time of actual armed rebellion against authority and government of the United States, and as a fit and necessary war measure for suppressing said rebellion, do, on this first day of January, in the year of our Lord one thousand eight hundred and sixty three, and in accordance with my purpose so to do publicly proclaimed for the full period of one hundred days, from the day first above mentioned, order and designate as the States and parts of States wherein the people thereof respectively, are this day in rebellion against the United States, the following, towit:

Arkansas, Texas, Louisiana, (except the Parishes of St. Bernard, Plaquemines, Jefferson, St. Johns, St. Charles, St. James Ascension, Assumption, Terrebonne, Lafourche, St. Mary, St. Martin, and Orleans, including the City of

*For a reproduction of the original document, see the endleaves.

New-Orleans) Mississippi, Alabama, Florida, Georgia, South-Carolina, North-Carolina, and Virginia, (except the fortyeight counties designated as West Virginia, and also the counties of Berkley, Accomac, Northampton, Elizabeth-City, York, Princess Ann, and Norfolk, including the cities of Norfolk and Portsmouth; and which excepted parts are, for the present, left precisely as if this proclamation were not issued.

And by virtue of the power, and for the purpose aforesaid, I do order and declare that all persons held as slaves within said designated States, and parts of States, are, and henceforward shall be free; and that the Executive government of the United States, including the military and naval authorities thereof, will recognize and maintain the freedom of said persons.

And I hereby enjoin upon the people so declared to be free to abstain from all violence, unless in necessary self-defence; and I recommend to them that, in all cases when allowed, they labor faithfully for reasonable wages.

And I further declare and make known that such persons of suitable condition, will be received into the armed service of the United States to garrison forts, positions, stations, and other places, and to man vessels of all sorts in said service.

And upon this act, sincerely believed to be an act of justice, warranted by the Constitution, upon military necessity, I invoke the considerate judgment of mankind, and the gracious favor of Almighty God.

In witness whereof, I have hereunto set my hand and caused the seal of the United States to be affixed.

Done at the City of Washington, this first day of January, in the year of our Lord one thousand eight hundred and sixty three, and of the Independence of the United States of America the eighty-seventh.

ABRAHAM LINCOLN
By the President
WILLIAM H. SEWARD,
Secretary of State.

There are several copies of the December 30 draft of the Emancipation Proclamation. The copies of Bates, Blair, Chase, and Seward are in the Library of Congress. The draft that the President worked with on December 31 and the morning of New Year's Day is considered the final manuscript draft. The principal parts of text are written in the President's hand. The two paragraphs from the Preliminary Proclamation were clipped from a printed copy and pasted on the President's draft "merely to save writing." The superscription and the formal closing are in the hand of a clerk in the Department of State. Later in the year Lincoln presented it to the ladies in charge of the Northwestern Fair in Chicago to be sold for the benefit of the Sanitary Commission. The President told the ladies that he had some desire to retain the paper, "but if it shall contribute to the relief or comfort of the soldiers that will be better." Thomas B. Bryan purchased it and presented it to the Soldiers Home in Chicago, of which he was president. It was destroyed in the Great Fire of 1871. Fortunately, four photographic copies of the original had been made. The official engrossed document is in the National Archives and follows Lincoln's original.[4]

There was no mention in the final draft of Lincoln's pet schemes of compensation and colonization. He had not abandoned them altogether, but in early 1863 he was not as optimistic about their success as he earlier had been. In the Preliminary Proclamation the President had said that he would declare slaves in designated areas to be "then, thenceforward, and forever free." In the final draft he was content to say that they "are, and henceforward shall be free." Perhaps the phrases meant the same, but the omission of "forever" in the final draft seemed to soften the harsh finality of the Proclamation. Again, after indicating in the Preliminary Proclamation that the government would recognize and maintain the freedom of the former slaves, the President promised that the government would "do no act or acts to repress such person, or any of them in any efforts they may make for their actual freedom." This last promise was omitted altogether from the final draft, perhaps as a result of the views expressed by Chase.

The President resisted the pleas of Chase not to make exceptions of parts of states. His view, supported by Attorney General Bates, was that he had promised to make exceptions of parts of states, and he wanted to keep his promise. An important consideration, moreover, was the view that in the prosecution of the war to save the Union, he would welcome the Confederate disaffection that the collapse and surrender of parts of states represented. It was good to have, say, New Orleans and the surrounding territory out of the fight. If the slaves in the remainder of Louisiana were set free, the act might help to crush the Confederate portion of the state and purchase some good will in the parts already in Union hands.

Nothing had been said in the Preliminary Proclamation about the use of black soldiers. In the preceding summer the Confiscation Act had authorized the President to use blacks in any way he saw fit, and there had been some limited use of them in noncombat capacities. In stating in the Proclamation itself that former slaves were to be received into the armed service, the President felt that he was using Congressional authority to strike a mighty blow against the Confederacy. For months Secretary of War Stanton had been urging this course of action. He was, therefore, immensely pleased with the Proclamation.

It was late afternoon before the Proclamation was ready for transmission to the press, diplomatic corps, government officials, and military officers. Earlier drafts were apparently available, and some use was made of them. The New York *Times* reported on January 1 that the Proclamation had been dispatched to the military the previous day.[5] The Washington *Star* carried the text of the Proclamation on New Year's Day, but it did not contain the correction in the subscription that the President had discovered just that morning. It was about 8 P.M. on January 1 when the transmission of the text over the telegraph wires began.

At the Government Printing Office the printers worked during the afternoon and evening of New Year's Day. They printed for the Department of State a two-page broadsheet containing the Proclamation. Within the next several days the Printing Office produced several other editions of the Proclamation for the Army, Navy, diplomatic corps, and others. By the beginning of the following week there seemed to be ample copies of the Proclamation to let the world know what Abraham Lincoln had done.

Young Edward Rosewater, scarcely twenty years old, had an exciting New Year's Day. He was a mere telegraph operator in the War Department; but he knew President Lincoln and had gone to the White House reception earlier that day and had greeted the President. When the President made his regular call at the telegraph office that evening young Rosewater was on duty and was more excited than ever. He greeted the President and went back to his work. The President walked over to see what Rosewater was sending out. It was the Emancipation Proclamation! If Rosewater was excited, the President seemed the picture of relaxation. After watching the young operator for a while, he went over to Eckert's desk, sat in his favorite chair, and gave his feet the proper elevation. He was soon joined by General Halleck and some others.[6] It was the end of long, busy, but perfect day.

Since the spring of 1862 the slaves of the District of Columbia had been free. The act of Congress of April 11, which was signed by the President after some hesitation, had been the first of the several emancipation acts passed by Congress. It was an uneasy emancipation, however. Blacks came in from Maryland and other border states, but the fugitive slave law was still in effect. Should they be returned? Some insisted that they should be, and some actually were returned. Contrabands were coming into the capital from Virginia, North Carolina, and other Confederate states. Their status had been the subject of much discussion since the beginning of the war when General Ben Butler declared runaway slaves "Contrabands of war." Perhaps the President's Proclamation would help clear the air.

The blacks of the District of Columbia did not wait until the President signed the Proclamation to begin their celebration. At noon on New Year's Day the contrabands gathered in front of the office of the superintendent of the camp,

Dr. B. D. Nichols, and "engaged in a variety of exercises appropriate to the day and to their condition." One of them led the group in singing "I'm a Free Man Now, Jesus Christ Made Me Free." Another took up the theme and began the ever popular "Go Down Moses." A woman then sang a song composed for the occasion, "There Will Be No More Task Masters," the others joining in the chorus. A Virginia contraband spoke feelingly on what it meant to be free. "I have worked by the month for six months . . . and the money is all my own; and I'll soon educate my children. But, brethren, don't be too free. . . . Don't lean on our master (pointing to Dr. Nichols). . . . You must depend on yourselves."

After a recess of several hours the group reassembled at 7 P.M. in the schoolhouse, with more than three hundred present. They sang and prayed and, then, the great moment. The text of the Emancipation Proclamation was available and Dr. Nichols read it to the assembled group. "Considerable interest was manifested when he stated that any of them who came from North Carolina were free, but on his enumerating the different portions in Virginia in which freedom was declared, the excitement was great in the assemblage, and as county by county was named, exclamations sprang from all quarters of the room. . . ." As Nichols called out the names of the Virginia counties that were excepted and as he omitted other counties, there were shouts from various parts of the house, "I am free!" He told them that they could now work for themselves, and he advised them not to ask too much. Begin with low wages and work up like white men. He told them that they were now like white men, and if called on would have to shoulder the muskets like them.

William Beverly, a Virginia contraband, offered a prayer imploring God to "prosper the work to be done in this land and country, and aid us by Thy . . . hand," and "Let Thy blessing rest on everything belonging to the President of the United States who has bestowed such gifts on us this night." George Payne, a tall, good-looking contraband from

Loudoun County, Virginia, told of the cruelty of his wife's former master. They lived fifteen miles from him, and her master had sold her and their children; and now he had been unable to locate them. "His heart had thumped when the proclamation was being read, wondering if Loudoun was included, Thanks be to God, Loudoun is free! Bless that man they call Mr. Lincoln for such a glorious proclamation."[7]

Meanwhile, Israel Bethel Church, presided over by the Reverend Henry M. Turner, was holding Washington's other major celebration. Turner himself went out to secure a copy of the Washington *Evening Star* that carried the text of the Proclamation. At the office of the *Star* the "first sheet run off with the Proclamation was grabbed by three of us, but some active young man got possession of it and fled. The next sheet was grabbed by several, and it was torn into tatters. The third sheet . . . was grabbed by several, but I succeeded in procuring so much of it as contained the Proclamation, and off I went for life and death."

Back at the church, Turner waved from the pulpit the newspaper that contained the good tidings. He began to read the document, but was so completely out of breath that he was unable to finish. He handed it to a Mr. Hinton who read it "with great force and clearness." This was the signal for the beginning of an unrestrained celebration characterized by men squealing, women fainting, dogs barking, and whites and blacks shaking hands.[8] The celebrations in Washington continued far into the night. In the Navy Yard, cannons began to roar and continued for some time. Lincoln was not alone in having a long day.

In the New York area the news of the Proclamation was received with mixed feelings. Blacks looked and felt happy, reported the New York *Times*, while abolitionists "looked glum, and grumbled with dissatisfaction because the unexpected proclamation was only given on account of military necessity. . . ."[9] The paper added that there were but few public demonstrations of joy. Within the week, however,

there were several large demonstrations in which prominent abolitionists took part. In Brooklyn, blacks held a large
New Year's Day celebration at Bridge Street Church, while
at Plymouth Church on the following Sunday, Henry Ward
Beecher preached a commemorative sermon to an overflow
audience. "The Proclamation may not free a single slave,"
he declared, "but it gives liberty a moral recognition."[10]

The big New York celebration was held on Monday
evening January 5 at the Cooper Union. In the spacious
hall, an overflow audience, two fifths of which was white,
struck "joyous notes of jubilee that echoed the edict of Negro emancipation." There were several speeches by whites
and blacks; but perhaps the climax was the speech by the
veteran abolitionist, Lewis Tappan, who "spoke touchingly
from a full heart." Looking back on several decades of fighting the slave power, Tappan felt that his investment in
money and energy had not been in vain. He looked to the
future when the black would have the opportunity to func-
tion as a citizen in American society. Music was inter-
spersed among the several addresses. Notable among the
renditions was the singing of the "New John Brown Song"
and the "Emancipation Hymn."[11]

The largest celebrations held anywhere were those held
in Boston on New Year's Day. In the late afternoon at the
Music Hall a veritable galaxy of leading literary figures
headed the list of distinguished citizens who gathered to
take notice of the climax of the fight that New England abolitionists had led for more than a generation. There were
John Greenleaf Whittier and Henry Wadsworth Long-
fellow, Oliver Wendell Holmes and Charles Eliot Norton,
Edward Everett Hale and Harriet Beecher Stowe, Francis
Parkman and Josiah Quincy. It was essentially a jubilee concert. The Philharmonic Orchestra, under the direction of
Carl Zerrahn, played the Fifth Symphony by Beethoven,
and a chorus sang Mendelssohn's "Hymn of Praise." For the
occasion, Ralph Waldo Emerson wrote the "Boston Hymn"
and read it to the audience.

The word of the Lord by night
To the watching Pilgrims came,
As they sat by the seaside,
And filled their hearts with flame.
. . . .

God said, I am tired of kings,
I suffer them no more;
Up to my ear the morning brings
The outrage of the poor.
. . . .

My angel,—his name is Freedom,—
Choose him to be your King;
He shall cut pathways east and west
And fend you with his wing.
. . . .

I will divide my goods;
Call in the wretch and slave:
None shall rule but the humble,
And none but Toil shall have.
. . . .

I break your bonds and masterships,
And I unchain the slave:
Free be his heart and hand henceforth
As wind and wandering wave.
. . . .

Up! and the dusky race
That sat in darkness long,—
Be swift their feet as antelopes,
And as behemoth strong.[12]

During the concert a man on the floor announced, "The President's Proclamation has been issued, and is now coming over the wires." A storm of enthusiasm followed such as had never before been seen from such an audience in the staid Music Hall. "Shouts arose, hats and handkerchiefs were waved, men and women sprang to their feet to give more energetic utterance to their joy." Three cheers were called for and given for Abraham Lincoln; then three more and then another three. Three cheers were called for and given for William Lloyd Garrison, the pioneer abolitionist leader. "A few hisses, immediately ceasing, were heard through this last applause, showing the presence of an unconverted minority."[13]

In the early evening, at a meeting sponsored by the Union Progressive Association, a large crowd gathered at the Tremont Temple to await the news that the President had signed the Proclamation. To speed the news of the signing, a line of messengers was stationed between the telegraph office and the platform of the Temple. Some of Boston's most distinguished citizens were absent, having "spent themselves" at the meeting at the Music Hall. Others, such as Julia Ward Howe, Wendell Phillips, and Bronson Alcott, were at the home of George L. Stearns for the unveiling of a bust of John Brown. Charles Sumner, still in Washington, did not receive his invitation in time to make the journey. But the gathering was not without its illustrious figures. Brief speeches were made by Judge Thomas Russell, Anna Dickinson, Attorney John S. Rock, the Reverend Leonard Grimes, William Wells Brown, J. Sella Martin, and Frederick Douglass.

Among the three thousand people assembled in Tremont Temple there were many who hoped, but doubted that the President would issue the final Proclamation. Their own feelings contributed to the natural anxiety that they all felt in waiting for the great moment. Douglass described the experience in the following words:

> *Eight, nine, ten o'clock came and went and still no word. A visible shadow seemed falling on the expected throng, which the confident utterances of the speakers sought in vain to dispel. At last, when patience was well-nigh exhausted, and suspense was becoming agony, a man (I think it was Judge Russell) with hasty step advanced through the crowd, and with a face fairly illumined with the news he bore, exclaimed in tones that thrilled all hearts, "It is coming!" "It is on the wires!"[14]*

Immediately the solemn meeting in the Temple was transformed into a wild and joyous celebration. There were all forms of expression, "from shouts of praise to sobs and tears." Finally a black preacher brought the throng together again by leading the singing of

> *Sound the land timbrel o'er Egypt's dark sea,*
> *Jehovah hath triumphed, his people are free.*

At midnight the group was required, under the contract, to vacate the Temple. As there was no disposition to disperse, the Reverend Leonard Grimes invited the crowd to continue the meeting in the Twelfth Baptist Church, of which he was pastor. Soon, the church was packed from the doors to the pulpit. It was almost dawn when the assemblage dispersed. Douglass pronounced it a "worthy celebration of the first step on the part of the nation in its departure from the thraldom of ages." Looking back on the glorious day in Boston the editor of the *Liberator* said, "The first day of January, 1863, has now taken rank with the fourth of July, 1776, in the history of this country. The Proclamation, though leaving much to be done in the future, clears our course from all doubt and our process from all uncertainty."

But the Boston celebration was not over. On January 3 Governor Andrew ordered a one-hundred gun salute to be fired in honor of the Proclamation and "as an official recognition of the justice and necessity, by the Commonwealth of Massachusetts, which was the first of the United States to secure equal rights to all its citizens." On Sunday, January 4, another Emancipation meeting was held at Music Hall, where the great orator of abolition, Wendell Phillips, spoke to an overflow audience. The Proclamation, he said, linked the cause of a great nation "to the throne of the Almighty, proclaiming Liberty as an act of justice, and abolishing a system found inconsistent with the perpetuity of the Republic."

Phillips was especially heartened by the President's failure to mention colonization in the final Proclamation. This greatly elevated its tone and position over that of the Preliminary Proclamation:

> *"Will you go away, if I venture to free you?" said the President on the twenty-second of September. "May I*

colonize you among the sickly deserts or the vast jungles
of South America?" On the first day of January, he says to
the same four million, "Let me colonize you in the forts of
the Union, and put rifles in your hands! (Applause). Give
us your hand to defend the perpetuity of the Union!"

Phillips said that to the whites the Proclamation was nothing but a step in the progress of a people, rich, prosperous, and independent. But to the black people it was "the sunlight scattering the despair of centuries. It is a voice like that of God, that gives the slave the right to work and to walk, the right to child and to wife. It is a word that makes the prayers of the poor and the victim the cornerstone of the Republic."[15]

There were celebrations all over the North on New Year's Day or during the following week. In Rochester, Columbus, Philadelphia, and Chicago, blacks hailed Lincoln's signing of the Proclamation as inaugurating the Year of Jubilee. In Albany, Buffalo, Pittsburgh, and several other cities one-hundred gun salutes were fired. In Salem the bells were rung, and a National Freedom Salute of thirty-four guns was given on the Common by a section of the artillery. At Milford, a large crowd gathered at Lyceum Hall to await the news of the Proclamation, while listening to speeches and music. When word came that the Proclamation had been signed, the town bells were rung and fifty guns were fired. At Hanover, New Hampshire, the students at Dartmouth rang the college bell for three hours. At most meetings resolutions were adopted in praise of the President and in support of the Union. The Year of Jubilee had an auspicious beginning.

In various parts of the South, blacks greeted the new Year with celebrations for the Proclamation. One of the largest was held at Norfolk, Virginia. At this bustling Atlantic port, incidentally, blacks were not set free by the Proclamation because the city was already in Union hands. At the time of their celebration the text of the Proclamation had not reached Norfolk, but under the terms of the statement of September 22 no one could have presumed that Norfolk slaves would be emancipated. This was an example, however, of what happened to slavery when Union forces won control of an area: slavery merely ceased to exist, the exceptions in the Emancipation Proclamation to the contrary notwithstanding. To celebrate their assumed freedom more than 4,000 blacks, "of all kinds and colors," formed a procession and, behind a band of drums and fifes, paraded through the principal streets of the city. They carried several Union flags and cheered loudly for the downfall of slavery. With a remarkable capacity for divining, the New York *Times* said it "was understood that they were celebrating the birthday of the Emancipation Proclamation."[16]

In another major Southern city in Union hands, New Orleans, the warm reception of the Proclamation by blacks *and* native whites excited much interest in the North. One editor observed that the Union supporters in New Orleans seemed to be more enthusiastic about the Emancipation Proclamation than some Union men in the North. This comment was caused by the report of a huge celebration meeting in New Orleans attended by blacks and whites, some of whom were lifelong slaveholders. After speeches appropriate to the occasion, the following resolution was unanimously passed:

> *We fully approve the war measure set out in the proclamation of the President, January 1, 1863, as one called for by the exigencies of the contest, consumating at once an act of justice to one class and, inflicting at the same time on another class persisting in rebellion, the blow best calculated to reduce them to obedience of the laws.*[17]

In South Carolina the Union forces had been in possession of the Sea Islands and the Port Royal area since November 1861. On March 16, 1862, the War Department established the Military Department of the South, with headquarters at Hilton Head, at the entrance of Port Royal Sound. It was at Hilton Head, in April 1862, that Major General David Hunter issued the military emancipation proclamation that was immediately rescinded by the President. Port Royal, nevertheless, became an important center into which hundreds of contrabands flocked. These former slaves became the object of solicitude on the part of numerous philanthropic groups in the North. Organizations such as the Educational Commission of Boston and the Port Royal Relief Association of Philadelphia sent supplies. White and black teachers established schools, thereby beginning one of the first systematic efforts to educate the freedmen.

Despite the fact that Port Royal was in Union hands, President Lincoln made no exception to it or to any part of South Carolina in the Proclamation. Slaves in the area were, therefore, presumably set free by the Proclamation. It would scarcely have made any difference, one way or the other. Emancipation had been in the air since the Hunter proclamation. Schools were thriving, and contrabands were conducting themselves as free men. Since September, General Rufus Saxton had been receiving South Carolina blacks into the armed services, and Thomas Wentworth Higginson arrived from Massachusetts in November to take command of the First South Carolina Volunteers. Port Royal blacks were, indeed, already free on January 1, 1863; and they seemed prepared to promote the freedom of their brothers in every way possible.

For weeks Port Royal had been preparing for the New Year's Day celebration of the Emancipation Proclamation. For Charlotte Forten, the cultivated young black woman who had come down to teach in the contraband school, it was "the most glorious day this nation has yet seen."[18] For a stylish black sergeant, it was truly a day of days. A year earlier he had been servant of a colonel in the Confederate Army. Now he had the privilege of saluting his own colonel, Thomas Wentworth Higginson.[19] About ten o'clock the people began to arrive by land and by water at Camp Saxton, near Beaufort. The multitude was chiefly black women, dressed gaily, and black men looking "peculiarly respectable." There were many white visitors, ladies on horseback and in carriages, superintendents and teachers, officers, and cavalrymen. Charlotte Forten came with the other teachers and special visitors from the Port Royal area. The black soldiers were marched to the neighborhood of the platform that was occupied by "ladies and dignitaries" and by the band of the Eighth Maine.

The actual Emancipation Day observances began at eleven thirty with a prayer by J. H. Fowler, chaplain of the first South Carolina Volunteers. Then Professor John C. Zachos, superintendent of Paris Island, read an ode that he had written for the occasion. This was followed by the reading of the Proclamation, presumably the Preliminary draft, by Dr. W. H. Brisbane, "a thing infinitely appropriate," a South Carolinian, who had emancipated his own slaves, addressing South Carolinians. The Reverend Mansfield French then presented to Colonel Higginson a stand of colors that he had brought from New York for the black regiment. The very moment that French finished his speech the black members of the audience began to sing, completely spontaneously, "My country, 'tis of thee." Higginson said that it was an incident "so simple, so touching, so utterly unexpected and startling, that I can scarcely believe it on recalling, though it gave the key-note of the whole day. . . . I never saw anything so electric; it made all other words cheap; it seemed the choked voice of a race at last unloosed."

Higginson was virtually speechless, but when he had composed himself he made an appropriate response. He received the flags and handed them to two black color guards, Sergeant Prince Rivers and Corporal Robert Sutton, both of whom spoke, "and very effectively." The regiment sang "Marching Along," and the people joined in singing "John Brown." There were other speeches and then a "slight collation" for which ten oxen had been roasted whole, and a dress parade. Higginson pronounced it a perfect day, "nothing but success." Charlotte Forten described it as a "grand, glorious day. The dawn of freedom, which it heralds may not break upon us at once; but it will surely come, and sooner, I believe, than we have ever dared hope before."[20] Nowhere in the United States was the celebration of the Emancipation Proclamation more gala, festive, or moving than at Camp Saxton, South Carolina.

Emancipation Day evoked reactions and comments that have continued down to the present. Few Americans in 1863 failed to respond, in some way, to Lincoln's history-making Proclamation. One will never know how the silent millions felt; but the reactions of the more articulate ones constituted a veritable flood that doubtless reflected the views of the many who had nothing to say. Even before the President issued the Proclamation some Americans reacted, in anticipation of the event. The Washington *National Republican* said on January 1 that the emancipation policy must be "cordially sustained by all patriotic citizens without regard to former differences of opinion. . . . Let bygones be bygones. Slavery is a thing of the past. It has no place in the future of America." On the following day it praised the President for announcing a policy to receive blacks into military service. "This is a most wise measure, as it will enable our armies to advance with undiminished numbers."[21]

Another Washington newspaper, the *Morning Chronicle*, was even more unqualified in its praise of the Proclamation. "President Lincoln now destroys the right arm of rebellion—African slavery." He had made available to the Union cause more than three million blacks to fight, man ships, and furnish accurate information concerning the enemy. He had destroyed the nightmare of a political power grown strong enough to threaten the life of the Union. While the emancipation of the slaves might lead to their eventual exodus from the United States the President's act was a "great moral landmark, a shrine at which future visionaries shall renew their vows, a pillar of fire which shall yet guide other nations out of the night of their bondage. . . . Abraham Lincoln . . . is entitled to the everlasting gratitude of a despised race enfranchised, the plaudits of a distracted country saved, and an inscription of undying fame in the impartial records of history."[22]

In New York, Horace Greeley greeted the Proclamation with his expected enthusiasm, but he had not lost his critical faculties. "Tennessee and southern Louisiana, where rebellion still rages, should not have been excepted, but let us not cavil." The slaves who had received the New Year's gift of liberty were more than three millions in number, he said. "They are debased by life-long servitude . . . but they are still human and love liberty. . . . This Proclamation makes them active, unsleeping enemies of the Slaveholders' Rebellion, and we trust will go far to lower its pride and diminish its power. We hail it as a great stride toward the restoration of the Union."[23] The New York *Times* declared that whatever may be the immediate results of the Proclamation, "it changes entirely the relations of the National Government to the institution of slavery." The *Times* regretted that the Proclamation was not issued in the form of a military order since, as commander-in-chief, the President could take slaves as well as horses and his action under such circumstances would surely be sustained by the Supreme Court.[24]

Boston's *Liberator* was beside itself. Naturally it would have been happier if the Proclamation had not been issued as a military necessity. But the corner had been turned; the editor was sure of it. And the death knell of slavery had been sounded. The issue of January 9 was largely given over to news about the Proclamation. Six poems, composed to commemorate the signing of the Proclamation, were carried in the paper. They were "Slave Songs" by Jane Ashby, "The Departed Year" by R., "John Brown's Avenger" by F. B. Gage, "Abraham Lincoln" by W. D. Gallagher, "Our President" by R. A. R., and "January First" by Almira Seymour. Two stanzas of the Seymour poem clearly depicted the feeling of the *Liberator*'s editor:

Hear it, ye Traitors with your sealed doom frantic,
Your own salvation's summons, could you read!
Hear it, across the Christo-born Atlantic
Oppressed, to hope! Oppressors, well to heed!

Catch it, ye echoes of the loftiest mountains!
Chant it, ye thunders of the wildest sea!
Angels and men! Shout from life's deepest fountains,
Today, Today, Columbia is free.

The Cincinnati *Daily Gazette* praised the President for taking the only proper course left to him. Since the Confederacy had rejected his warning and elected to continue the war, he was forced to free the slaves. "In the struggle for the national existence these blacks are unavoidably a power on one side or another. There is no neutrality for them." Since blacks in the power of the rebels "are forced to aid them in treason, it follows that when men are engaged in treason they lose all right to hold other persons in subjection."[25] This was the general tenor of the section of the press that spoke favorably of the Proclamation. The emphasis was on the military necessity of the measure, with a suggestion, here and there, of the moral necessity of issuing the Proclamation.

The newspapers that were critical of the Preliminary Proclamation reacted unfavorably to the statement of January 1. The *National Intelligencer,* that had doubted the legality and utility of any such Proclamation, regarded the form of the final draft "unfortunate." The theory of executive power on which it proceeds "involves a political solecism of the gravest character, and on which, without sacrificing the *substance* of his decree, the President might have avoided by adopting a different style of language." The *Intelligencer* would have preferred Lincoln to hold and treat all slaves as free instead of declaring all slaves free. Whatever may be the theoretical objections to the Proclamation, "we do not perceive that, while the war lasts, the patrons of slavery have anything to complain of so far as regards the practical operation of the decree, which, if powerless to destroy slavery outside the range of our armies, is expressly designed to shelter slavery in one of the slaveholding States which is still the theatre of military operations."[26]

The Democratic press of New York was especially critical of the Proclamation. Even before the editor of the *World* read the text of the final draft he declared that if it were based on legal authority it would be "resplendent with moral grandeur"; but it was not even justified by the laws of war. After the Proclamation was issued he called it "clearly unconstitutional and wholly void unless sustainable as a war measure. A war measure it clearly is not, inasmuch as the previous success of the war is the only thing that can give it validity."[27] The *Herald*, apparently competing with the *World* in their total rejection of the Proclamation, said it was the "last card of the abolition Jacobins . . . unnecessary, unwise and ill-timed, impracticable, outside of the constitution and full of mischief." Predominant public opinion in the North, the editor concluded, regarded extreme abolition measures as "possibly destroying the Union instead of saving it."[28]

Few papers were as vehemently critical of the Proclamation as the anti-Administration Boston *Courier*. Its editor called the issuance of the Proclamation "stupendous folly," and an outright invitation to crimes and horrors unexampled in the history of the world. The editor declared that if such consequences come, Lincoln, Seward, and the other members of the Administration would be responsible. Then, the editor delivered his final blow:

> *We are amazed that he should venture to invoke the favor of Almighty God upon a proceeding, which, if effectual at all . . . would consign millions of God's accountable creatures to slaughter, and to be the victims of every brutal passion which can infuriate the human breast.*[29]

The President could hardly have been any more surprised at the strictures of the *World*, the *Herald*, and the *Courier* than he was at the praise of the *Tribune*, the Washington *Chronicle* and the Cincinnati *Gazette*. Indeed, having reached the decision after much deliberation and having weighed the several possible consequences, the President was impervious if not indifferent to national press reaction. This also seemed to be his attitude toward individuals or groups who commented on the Proclamation. He was confident that he had done the right thing, and he was much too busy to fret over adverse reactions. When General John A. McClernand expressed regret over the Proclamation, Lincoln replied, simply, "broken eggs can not be mended. I have issued the emancipation proclamation, and I can not retract it."[30]

There were scattered criticisms that came to the attention of the President. He never undertook to reply to them. In Congress Henry Grider of Kentucky said that there was "no grant of power to the Federal authority of any of its departments . . . to extinguish African slavery in any way, anywhere, by any right action of the General Government. . . ." He thought it absurd and illegal to seize the property of individuals "indiscriminately loyal and disloyal, guilty and not guilty, without a trial." His colleague, Jesse Lazear of Pennsylvania, did not use nearly so many words, but was no less critical when he pronounced the Proclamation to be "pregnant with more evil than any single act done by one man."[31] In New York, Governor Horatio Seymour feared that the new policy would convert the government into a military despotism, while Governor Robinson of Kentucky was certain that emancipation was an act of usurpation that would fire the South with "inextinguishable hatred."[32]

The criticisms in January lacked the punch of those in the previous September. If the Administration's opponents argued for the illegality of the Proclamation, they found difficulty in convincing anyone that the President's military powers did not extend to action against slavery. If the abolitionists saw insufficient appreciation in the Proclamation for the moral wrong of slavery, they knew all too well that things were now going their way. As Wendell Phillips said in late January, "No one worth minding now doubts or debates about the emancipation of slaves."[33] The President could afford to stand aside and pay little heed to the critics of emancipation. Their actions had become distinctly rear guard.

There was no reason to expect that the Confederate states would accept the Proclamation in indifferent silence. Lincoln could hardly have expected it; and no other Union leader who had any understanding of the temper and attitude of the Confederates could have been surprised at the vigorous rejection of the Proclamation by Southern people as well as by Jefferson Davis and his Administration. It was the "most startling political crime, the most stupid political blunder, yet known in American history," the Richmond *Examiner* declared. The paper was then pleased to conclude that the Proclamation would have a salutary effect on the people of the South. "It shuts the door of retreat and repentance on the weak and the timid."[34] The Richmond *Whig* did not dignify the Proclamation by discussing it. It merely reprinted the text of the Proclamation under the caption, "The Latest 'Bull' from Lincoln," and said that it was a part of the history of the times.[35]

In January 1863, Confederate newspapers were not nearly so vociferous in their condemnation or even their comment as they had been in September 1862. Some printed the Proclamation without comment. Some made no mention of it at all. They did not seem nearly so confident in January as they had been in September that the Proclamation was of no consequence. There were some editors, however, that scored the President's action in the manner that the Richmond papers had done. After announcing that the President had issued the Proclamation, an editor in Augusta, Georgia, said that it had not changed anything significantly. "We see no portentous signs of calamity, either in the heavens or on earth. The sun is not darkened, nor the moon turned into blood." He observed that the Northern people would not succeed in pulling down the pillars of the institution of slavery; and in attempting to do so they would merely bring ruin on themselves. "Whom God wishes to destroy he first deprives of reason." The Proclamation was an indication of the way in which the North was proceeding to bring about its own destruction.[36]

In his Message to the Confederate Congress on January 12, 1863, Jefferson Davis took cognizance of the Proclamation by indicating that it was printed in public journals of the North that had been received in Richmond. He stated clearly his low estimate of the Lincoln measure:

> We may well leave it to the instincts of that common humanity which a beneficent Creator has implanted in the breasts of our fellow-men of all countries to pass judgment on a measure by which several millions of human beings of an inferior race, peaceful and contented laborers in their sphere, are doomed to extermination, while at the same time they are encouraged to a general assassination of their masters by the insidious recommendation "to abstain from violence unless in necessary self-defense."

Davis then branded the Proclamation as the "most execrable measure recorded in the history of guilty man" and said that his own detestation of its authors was tempered only by "the profound rage which it discloses."

Davis's own profound rage was revealed in his announcement that he would deliver to state officials all commissioned officers of the United States that may be captured. They were then to be dealt with "in accordance with the laws of those states providing for the punishment of criminals engaged in exciting servile insurrection." He said that he would continue to treat enlisted soldiers as "unwilling instruments in the commission of these crimes, and shall direct their discharge and return to their homes on the proper and usual parole." He said that the Proclamation clearly revealed the base motives and intentions of the Lincoln Administration. It merely vindicated the sagacity of the people of the Confederacy in perceiving the uses to which the Republicans intended from the beginning to apply their power. It also indicated there was no longer any reason to entertain the hope that the North and South could become reconciled. "A restoration of the union has been rendered forever impossible by the adoption of a measure which from its very nature neither admits of retraction nor can coexist with union."[37]

There can be no doubt that the Southern people were animated to desperate exertion by the Proclamation. There were few statements by their President that they endorsed more heartily than his excoriation of the Emancipation Proclamation. After mid-January there was much talk of treating Union officers as Davis had suggested. Although there was never a formal adoption of the policy by Congress or the War Department, the recurring discussion of the possibility suggests the deep feeling on the matter that many Confederates had.

First and foremost the Proclamation was a military measure. The Washington government expected to undermine the Confederate war effort by relieving slaves of their obligation to serve the Confederate cause. It also hoped to receive as many of these former slaves as possible into the armed services of the United States. It became the peculiar responsibility of the military establishment to disseminate information about the proclamation over as wide an area as possible, as early as possible. Presumably an early draft of the final Proclamation was in the hands of some of the military even before the President signed it.[38] If so, no official action was taken by the Army until January 2. On that date the War Department issued General Orders No. 1, a three-page document containing the Proclamation. The Department printed fifteen thousand copies and distributed them in the following manner:

Bureaus	2,000
States, generals, posts, regiments, etc.	500
Cumberland Department	3,000
Department of the Gulf	1,200
Department of Missouri	1,000
Department of the Middle	800
Department of Tennessee	500
Department of Washington	400
Department of the East	300

The remainder went to the following Departments: Ohio, South, Virginia, North Carolina, North West, New Mexico, Pacific, Oregon (District), Susquehanna, Monongahela, West Virginia, and St. Mary's (District). On January 14 the Navy distributed its own edition of the Proclamation among its personnel. By this time it may be concluded that the military was well informed.

It is not possible to know the prevailing reaction of the average soldier to the Emancipation Proclamation. Some were willing to fight and die for Union but not for emancipation. For others, as Bell Wiley has suggested, the rallying cry became "Union and Freedom."[39] Still others were delighted with the prospect that blacks would now be permitted to share in the heavy burden of fighting the Confederacy. Perhaps the reaction of the soldier was not very important so long as he contributed to the destruction of the Confederacy by spreading the news among the slaves that they were free.

The manner in which slaves learned of the Emancipation Proclamation has been the subject of discussion for a hundred years. A few of them read about it and told others. Some learned about it by hearing whites discuss it among themselves. Many learned it from Union soldiers who spread the news as they took possession of Confederate territory. A most effective means of communicating the news was by the mysterious "grapevine" telegraph by which slaves passed along any news that came to their attention. Booker T. Washington said that during his slave childhood his elders seemed to be completely and accurately informed about the great national questions. They knew that their freedom would be the one great result of the war, if the Northern armies were successful.[40] After the Proclamation they were more certain than ever.

Perhaps a few slaves learned of the Proclamation from their own masters. Elizabeth Johnston has written an idealized account of such an incident at Ashley Hall in Kentucky. It was Christmas, 1862, and when his slaves came to the big house for their gifts and toddy, Colonel John Montgomery Ashley spoke to his assembled slaves. He told them that he had a message for them from a friend, "a great and good man—Abraham Lincoln, President of the United States." He told them that although it was an exciting message, they should remain quiet until he had finished. Then he read slowly and impressively the Preliminary Emancipation Proclamation. He indicated that Kentucky was not included but, "as there is not a doubt that freedom will be granted to your entire people, I have taken occasion to place the matter before you a little in advance."

Ashley said he wanted the slaves to begin thinking of their future. They would remain where they were and as they were for the present. When the President or Congress extended freedom to Kentucky they would then be free. If any decided to remain with him he would employ them as free laborers. At the end of his talk, there were cries, screams, shouts, and sobs and much laughter. The Ashley slaves had only two more years to wait.[41]

One suspects that the vast majority of the slaves knew of the Proclamation by the end of January 1863. On Magnolia Plantation in Mississippi, slaves declined to work on Christmas Day, 1862, saying that, having never had a chance to keep it before, "they would avail themselves of the privilege now, they thought." At Port Gibson, in February, a citizen complained to the Governor of Mississippi that blacks were under no restraint and were acting as they pleased.[42] Whenever the word reached an area or, better still, whenever the Army reached an area, blacks began to exercise some of the privileges of free people. It was this post-Proclamation conduct as well as some early evidences of insubordination that led Wiley to conclude that "disorder and unfaithfulness on the part of the Negroes were far more common than postwar commentators have usually admitted."[43]

The Army was leaving nothing for granted. Not only was it doing what it could to make good the freedom that the Proclamation promised, but it was seeking recruits among the former slaves. The office of the Adjutant General soon had the machinery established for the enlistment of blacks into the segregated unit known as the Bureau of Colored Troops. Recruiters were dispatched not only to Northern communities but also to areas in the South that had been taken from the Confederates. Recruiters proclaimed freedom with posters, speeches, and in other ways.[44] The recruiters succeeded in enlisting 134,000 black soldiers in the slave states as compared with 52,000 from the free states, where, incidentally the black population was much smaller. Blacks had, thus, not only become free by virtue of the Confiscation Act, the Emancipation Proclamation, and the force of the Union Army, but they had begun to fight for freedom by the spring of 1863.

If the Proclamation was a war measure, it was designed not only to strengthen the position of the Union in its total prosecution of the war at home, but also to defeat as far as possible the efforts of the Confederacy abroad. The entire Administration had become acutely aware, by the end of 1862, of the importance of eliminating any disposition on the part of other countries to recognize or give assistance to the Confederacy. Already the clandestine assistance that the British had given Confederate privateers had seriously injured Union shipping. Added to this was the expressed admiration for the Confederacy on the part of some highly placed British and French government officials. It was enough to disturb responsible leaders much less sensitive than Lincoln and Seward.

Much of the British press criticized the Proclamation of January 1, but some did so in a less strident voice than they had criticized the Preliminary Proclamation. The London *Times* found "little homage to principle" in the document. But even the *Times* was compelled to admit that any effort to emancipate any portion of the slave population, "however tardily, reluctantly, and partially made," must have an effect on the opinion of mankind.[45] The *Saturday Review* was not as conciliatory. It was a call to servile war or it was nothing, the editor declared. The President, in issuing the Proclamation, closed the door on all possibility of peaceful reunion. Even more discouraging was the fact that British abolitionists were supporting "a rousing agitation on behalf of the divine right of insurrection and massacre."[46]

In a similar though more conciliatory vein the *Spectator* asserted that the President had failed to secure the European sympathy that a bold appeal would have done. Then, it added, "Every part of its act, rude and imperfect as its conception may be, tends to raise human beings in the scale of humanity, to increase their capacity of happiness, to carry one step farther the ideas for which we English profess to stand ready to risk our lives."[47] John Ruskin was not so certain about this. He thought that it was "the most miserable idiocy" to mix up the fight for dominion with a fight for liberty. "As for your precious Proclamation," he wrote Charles Eliot Norton, "if I had it here—there's a fine north wind blowing and I would give it to the first boy I met to fly it as his kite's tail."[48]

Official Britain could not afford to take the Proclamation as lightly as Ruskin did. Lord Russell, the Foreign Minister, said that the Proclamation "appears to be of a very strange nature." At once it made slavery illegal in the Confederacy and legal in the union. "There seems to be no declaration of a principle adverse to slavery in this Proclamation. It is a measure of war, and a measure of war of a very questionable kind."[49] Perhaps it was a questionable measure, but the Foreign Minister was discovering that British foreign policy was not being shaped exclusively in his office. He began to realize, moreover, that pro-Confederate sentiment and policy in Britain had passed its apex. And the Emancipation Proclamation was an important factor in the change that was taking place.

Even before the end of the Hundred Days, British antislavery supporters of the North were increasing in numbers and influence. "Beginning with the last week of December, 1862, and increasing in volume in each succeeding month, there took place meeting after meeting at which strong resolutions were passed enthusiastically endorsing the issue of the emancipation proclamation and pledging sympathy to the cause of the North."[50] It is estimated that no less that fifty-six meetings were held between December 30, 1862, and March 20, 1863. If these meetings were made up of "nobodies" as the *Times* claimed, the aggregate of them constituted a mighty voice in the land. Richard Cobden said that the announcement of the emancipation policy aroused the old antislavery feeling in England, and the great rush of the people to the public meetings showed how wide and deep the sympathy for personal freedom still was in the hearts of the people.[51] Henry Adams, whose father was the United States Minister to Britain, wrote from London that "The Emancipation Proclamation has done more for us here than all our former victories and all our diplomacy."[52]

Charles Francis Adams, the United States Minister to Britain, was keenly aware of the importance of the emancipation meetings, and he kept the Department of State well informed regarding them. He transmitted full accounts of the meetings together with copies of the resolutions they adopted. The Sheffield meeting of December 31 congratulated Lincoln for his stand for freedom and wished him

"God-speed in the endeavor to consummate the great and good work of freedom and union." It then added, "We deeply regret that any of our countrymen should have displayed a feeling of sympathy with those in America who are fighting to establish an oligarchical government on the basis of enslavement of a weak and defenceless race. . . ." On January 15, 1863, the Emancipation Society of London met and passed a resolution expressing profound satisfaction with the news that the President had issued the Proclamation. It further stated that it understood that the limitations of the Proclamation constituted an act of submission to the Constitution and reflected no indifference on the part of the President to the injustice and evil of slavery in other districts of the Union.

There were similar meetings at Leeds, Manchester, Glasgow, Newcastle upon Tyne, Edinburgh, and scores of other British towns and cities. The resolutions praised a policy that would "seal the doom of the sum of all villainies," that reflected the "successive triumphs of anti-slavery sentiment in the United States," and that demonstrated the courage and capacity of the government in Washington to deal with a most difficult situation. "The great heart of the British people beats, we assure, true to freedom," the Glasgow resolution concluded.[53] Small wonder that Adams could report with satisfaction that in Britain "the current of sentiment continues to run strongly in the direction lately taken." He correctly evaluated the effect of this sentiment when he concluded, "It appears to have considerably modified the tone of most persons in authority."[54] Lyons realized that the Lincoln government appreciated this fact. He told his government in London that the new confidence in Washington caused government officials to be unreasonable and presumptuous in dealing with us."[55]

On the Continent, reaction to the Proclamation was not nearly so adverse as it had been to the announcement in September. From Belgium, Henry Sanford said that the United States was gaining steadily in Europe as a result of the action against slavery. In Brussels, he reported, the "principal organs of public opinion, liberal and catholic, are friendly to us. . . ."[56] In the Netherlands, despite the adverse reports of its minister to the United States regarding Lincoln and his Proclamation, the Dutch people generally approved the emancipation policy.[57] France's reaction was equivocal. The Chamber of Deputies refused to approve a resolution supporting emancipation on the ground that "such language did not become a neutral power."[58] But the Protestant Pastors of France vigorously denounced slavery; and in an Appeal of February 12, 1863, they called on ministers of all evangelical denominations of England, Scotland, and Ireland to join them in stirring up a "great and peaceful demonstration of sympathy for the black race, so long enchained and debased by Christian nations."[59]

On the whole the Proclamation evoked favorable response in Spain. Gustavus Koener, the United States Minister, reported in late January that he had presented a copy to the Spanish government and it was cordially received.[60] One newspaper, *España*, called it a "first rate political blunder," but another, *El Diario*, said that as a result of the Proclamation, slavery was doomed regardless of the outcome of the war. Surely, after January 1863, Spain did not entertain any serious thought of pursuing a pro-Confederate policy. The more liberal-minded Spaniards welcomed the Proclamation as a weapon in their drive to end slavery in the Spanish colonies.[61]

In Italy interest in the Proclamation ran high. Pope Pius IX, who in the fall had urged Archbishop John J. Hughes of New York and Archbishop Jean Marie Odin of New Orleans to attempt a mediation between North and South, had not given up hope. But he was not as optimistic about a reconciliation as he had been earlier.[62] Massimo d'Azeglio, the sensitive and articulate Governor of Milan, was not completely satisfied with the Proclamation or with Lincoln. Czar Alexander II, he said, was greater than Lincoln, for while Lincoln only freed the slaves of his enemies the Czar freed the slaves of his friends.[63] There was, however, some unqualified praise for the Proclamation. *Il Giornale di Roma* said it was not only a great measure that was entirely legal but it would in time promote peace.[64] Garibaldi, the great leader of unification, took time out to congratulate Lincoln, "Pilot of Liberty" and to greet the former slaves with the declaration that "the freemen of Italy kiss the glorious marks of your chains."[65]

The Russians, having so recently emancipated their own serfs, were particularly interested in the emancipation policy in the United States. Perhaps their general reaction was reflected in the editorial comment by the St. Petersburg *Vedomosti*, which found the Proclamation important "regardless of the motivations or necessity, therefore, a great benevolent deed."[66] The Czar was a bit more reserved in his praise. Several years later he told his American friend, Wharton Barker, that he did more for the Russian serf "in giving him land as well as personal liberty, than America did for the Negro slave set free by the Proclamation of President Lincoln." The Russian ruler was at a loss, he said, "to understand how you Americans could have been so blind as to leave the Negro slave without tools to work out his salvation."[67] This statement, made in 1879, reflected the benefit of both wisdom in general and knowledge of the years of reconstruction in particular.

5 Victory More Certain

T he character of the Civil War could not possibly have been the same after the President issued the Emancipation Proclamation as it had been before January 1, 1863. During the first twenty months of the war, no one had been more careful than Lincoln himself to define the war merely as one to save the Union. He did this not only because such a definition greatly simplified the struggle and kept the border states fairly loyal, but also because he deeply felt that this was the only legitimate basis for prosecuting the war. When, therefore, he told Horace Greeley that if he could save the Union without freeing a single slave he made the clearest possible statement of his fundamental position. And he was holding to this position despite the fact that he had written the first draft of the Emancipation Proclamation at least six weeks before he wrote his reply to Greeley's famous "Prayer of Twenty Millions."

Lincoln saw no contradiction between the contents of his reply to Greeley and the contents of the Emancipation Proclamation. For he had come to the conclusion that in order to save the Union he must emancipate *some* of the slaves. His critics were correct in suggesting that the Proclamation was a rather frantic measure, an act of last resort.

By Lincoln's own admission it was, indeed, a desperate act; for the prospects of Union success were not bright. He grabbed at the straw of a questionable victory at Antietam as the occasion for issuing the Preliminary Proclamation. If anything convinced him in late December that he should go through with issuing the final Proclamation, it was the ignominious defeat of the Union forces at Fredericksburg. *Something* needed to be done. Perhaps the Emancipation Proclamation would turn the trick!

The language of the Proclamation revealed no significant modification of the aims of the war. Nothing was clearer than the fact that Lincoln was taking the action under his authority "as Commander-in-Chief of the Army and Navy." The situation that caused him to take the action was that there was an "actual armed rebellion against the authority and government of the United States." He regarded the Emancipation Proclamation, therefore, as "a fit and necessary war measure for suppressing said rebellion." In another place in the Proclamation he called on the military and naval authorities to recognize and maintain the freedom of the slaves. Finally the President declared, in the final paragraph of the Proclamation, that the measure was "warranted by the Constitution upon military necessity." This was, indeed, a war measure, conceived and promulgated to put down the rebellion and save the Union.

Nevertheless, both by what it said and what it did not say, the Proclamation greatly contributed to the significant shift in 1863 in the way the war was regarded. It recognized the right of emancipated slaves to defend their freedom. The precise language was that they should "abstain from all violence, unless in necessary self-defence." It also provided that former slaves could now be received into the armed services. While it was clear that they were to fight to save the Union, the fact remained that since their own fate was tied to that of the Union, they would also be fighting for their own freedom. The black who, in December 1862, could salute his own colonel instead of blacking the boots of a Confederate colonel, as he had been doing a year earlier, had a stake in the war that was not difficult to define. However loyal to the Union the black troops were—and they numbered some 190,000 by April 1865—one is inclined to believe that they were fighting primarily for freedom for themselves and their brothers in the months that followed the issuance of the Emancipation Proclamation.

Despite the fact that the President laid great stress on the issuance of the Proclamation as a military necessity, he did not entirely overlook the moral and humanitarian significance of the measure. And even in the document itself he gave some indication of his appreciation of this particular dimension that was, in time, to eclipse many other considerations. He said that the emancipation of the slaves was "sincerely believed to be an act of justice." This conception of emancipation could hardly be confined to the slaves in states or parts of states that were in rebellion against the United States on January 1, 1863. It must be recalled, moreover, that in the same sentence that he referred to emancipation as an "act of justice" he invoked "the considerate judgment of mankind and the gracious favor of Almighty God." This raised the Proclamation above the level of just another measure for the effective prosecution of the war. And, in turn, the war became more than a war to save the integrity and independence of the Union. It became also a war to promote the freedom of mankind.

Throughout the previous year the President had held to the view that blacks should be colonized in some other part of the world. And he advanced this view with great vigor wherever and whenever possible. He pressed the Cabinet and Congress to accept and implement his colonization views, and he urged blacks to realize that it was best for all concerned that they should leave the United States. It is not without significance that Lincoln omitted from the Emancipation Proclamation any reference to colonization. It seems clear that the President had abandoned hope of gaining support for his scheme or of persuading blacks to leave the only home they knew. Surely, moreover, it would have been a most incongruous policy as well as an ungracious act to have asked blacks to perform one of the highest acts of citizenship—fighting for their country—and then invite them to leave. Thus, by inviting blacks into the armed services and omitting all mention of colonization, the President indicated in the Proclamation that blacks would enjoy a status that went beyond mere freedom. They were to be free persons, fighting for their *own* country, a country in which they were to be permitted to remain.

The impact of the Proclamation on slavery and blacks was profound. Blacks looked upon it as a document of freedom, and they made no clear distinction between the areas affected by the Proclamation and those not affected by it. One has the feeling that the interest of the contrabands in Washington in seeing whether their home counties were excepted or included in the Proclamation was an academic interest so far as their own freedom was concerned. After all, they had proclaimed their own freedom and had put themselves beyond the force of the slave law or their masters. The celebration of the issuance of the Proclamation by thousands of blacks in Norfolk illustrates the pervasive influence of the document. President Lincoln had said that Norfolk slaves were not emancipated by his Proclamation. Norfolk blacks, however, ignored the exception and welcomed the Proclamation as the instrument of their own deliverance.

Slavery, in or out of the Confederacy, could not possibly have survived the Emancipation Proclamation. Slaves themselves, already restive under their yoke and walking off the plantation in many places, were greatly encouraged upon learning that Lincoln wanted them to be free. They proceeded to oblige him. There followed what one authority has called a general strike and another has described as widespread slave disloyalty throughout the Confederacy.[1] Lincoln understood the full implications of the Proclamation. That is one of the reasons why he delayed issuing it as

long as he did. Once the power of the government was enlisted on the side of freedom in one place, it could not suc-
cessfully be restrained from supporting freedom in some
other place. It was too fine a distinction to make. Not even
the slaveholders in the excepted areas could make it. They
knew, therefore, that the Emancipation Proclamation was
the beginning of the end of slavery for them. Many of them
did not like it, but the realities of the situation clearly indicated what the future had in store for them.

The critics of the Lincoln Administration stepped up
their attack after January 1, 1863, because they fully appreciated the fact that the Proclamation changed the character
of the war. Orestes A. Brownson, Clement L. Vallandigham,
William C. Fowler, Samuel S. Cox, and others insisted that
the Proclamation represented a new policy that made impossible any hasty conclusion of the struggle based on a
compromise. The President had become the captive of the
abolitionists who had persuaded him to change the war
aims from preservation of the Union to abolition of slavery.
Some of them, such as Vallandigham, were proslavery and
openly defended the "peculiar institution" against what
they called unconstitutional interference. Others, such as
Fowler, felt that the question of slavery was extraneous and
the introduction of emancipation into the picture was an act
so loathsome as to be virtually criminal. All agreed that the
Proclamation transformed the war into something to which
they were even more bitterly opposed than they had been
to the war to save the Union.

If the abolitionists had gained ascendancy in the councils of the President, they were not altogether satisfied with
the results of their influence. For months on end, they had
been imploring the President to abolish slavery. "Stevens,
Sumner, and Wilson simply haunt me with their importuni-
ties for a Proclamation of Emancipation," Lincoln complained to a friend in 1862. Outright emancipation of all the
slaves, without compensation or colonization and without
apologies for it as a military necessity, was what the aboli-

tionists wanted. "Patch up a compromise now," warned Thaddeus Stevens, "leaving this germ of evil and it will soon again overrun the whole South, even if you free three fourths of the slaves. Your peace would be a curse. You would have expended countless treasures and untold lives in vain." Many abolitionists agreed with Stevens, when he said, in early September 1862, that no one in the government seemed to have the moral courage to take the necessary steps to abolish slavery.[2]

In the light of the demands they had been making, the language of the Emancipation Proclamation could hardly have been the source of unrestrained joy on the part of the abolitionists. The Proclamation did not represent the spirit of "no compromise" that had characterized their stand for a generation. There was no emancipation in the border states, with which the abolitionists had so little patience. Parts of states that were under Union control were excepted, much to the dismay of the abolitionists, whose view was ably set forth by Chase. Obviously, the President was not completely under their sway, despite the claims of numerous critics of the Administration. For the most part, the Proclamation represented Lincoln's views. It was in no sense the result of abolitionist dictation.

And yet, when the Proclamation finally came, the abolitionists displayed a remarkable capacity for accommodating themselves to what was, from their point of view, an obvious compromise. Some of them took credit for the begrudging concessions that the compromise represented. They were wrung, Wendell Phillips told a Boston audience, "from reluctant leaders by the determined heart of the masses."[3] A few weeks later he said to a group of New Yorkers, "Possess your souls in patience, not as having already attained, not as if we were already perfect, but because the whole nation, as one man, has for more than a year set its face Zionward. Ever since September 22nd of last year, the nation has turned its face Zionward, and ever since Burnside drew his sword in Virginia, we have moved toward that point. . . . We have found at last the method, and we are in earnest."[4]

Other abolitionists had even fewer reservations. Thaddeus Stevens praised Lincoln's Proclamation. It contained "precisely the principles which I had advocated," he told his Pennsylvania constituents.[5] For thirty years William Lloyd Garrison had never been known to make concessions as far as slavery was concerned. Yet, he declared the Emancipation Proclamation to be a measure that should take its place along with the Declaration of Independence as one of the nation's truly important historic documents. Frederick Douglass, the leading black abolitionist, said that the Proclamation changed everything. "It gave a new direction to the councils of the Cabinet, and to the conduct of the national arms." Douglass realized that the Proclamation did not extend liberty throughout the land, as the abolitionists hoped, but he took it "for a little more than it purported, and saw in its spirit a life and power far beyond its letter. Its meaning to me was the entire abolition of slavery," he concluded, "and I saw that its moral power would extend much further."[6]

Ralph Waldo Emerson, who read his "Boston Hymn" at the Emancipation celebration in the Music Hall, was not the only articulate enemy of slavery who was moved to write verse to commemorate the historic event. John Greenleaf Whittier, widely regarded as the poet of abolition, wrote "The Proclamation" in the fall of 1862 and circulated it among friends. Charlotte Forten read it to a group at Port Royal on New Year's Day, and it was published in the *Atlantic* in February. He recorded his great satisfaction with the Proclamation in the following lines:

> *O dark, sad millions, patiently and dumb*
> *Waiting for God, your hour, at last, has come*
> *And Freedom's Song*
> *Breaks the long silence of your night of wrong!*
>
> *Arise and flee! Shake off the vile restraint*
> *of ages! but, like Ballymena's saint,*

The oppressor spare,
Heap only on his head the coals of prayer!

Go forth, like him! like him, return again,
To bless the land whereon in bitter pain
Ye toiled at first,
And heal with freedom what your slavery cursed![7]

Oliver Wendell Holmes had not been as active as Whittier in the crusade against slavery. But his standing both as a citizen and as a man of letters could hardly be surpassed. His abolitionist sympathies were well known, and it could hardly have been a surprise that he joined Emerson, Whittier, and others in praise of the Proclamation. In his "Choose You This Day Whom Ye Will Serve," he said,

Yes, tyrants, you hate us, and fear while you hate
The self-ruling, chain-breaking, throne-shaking State!
The night-birds dread morning,—your instinct is true,—
The day-star of Freedom brings midnight for you!

Whose God will ye serve, O Ye rulers of men?
Will ye build you new shrines
in the slave-breeders den?
Or bow with the children of light, as they call
On the Judge of the Earth and the Father of All?[8]

The enthusiasm of the abolitionists was greater than that of a group that had reached the conclusion that half a loaf was better than none. Their initial reaction of dissatisfaction with the Preliminary Proclamation had been transformed into considerable pleasure over the edict of January 1. Most of them seemed to agree with Douglass that the Proclamation had, indeed, changed everything. Even if the Proclamation did not free a single slave, as Henry Ward Beecher admitted, it gave liberty a moral recognition. It was a good beginning, the most significant step that had been taken in a generation of crusading. It was only a beginning, however, as the delegation of antislavery leaders from Boston indicated to Lincoln when they visited him in late January.

Wendell Phillips, Samuel Gridley Howe, Elizur Wright, Moncure Conway, and several other crusading abolitionists from Boston were greatly distressed over the covert opposition in high places to the Emancipation Proclamation. They had learned, for example, that Governor Stanly of North Carolina was continuing to denounce it and all who believed in it. They resolved that the best thing to do was to place the matter before the President. On Sunday evening, January 25, they went, in the company of their Senator, Henry Wilson, to the White House. The President received them graciously. Phillips told the President how delighted they were with the Proclamation. He added that they wondered whether, in the face of open hostility to it in pro-slavery quarters, it was being "honestly carried out by the nation's agent and generals in the South." Lincoln said that the lack of military successes was the principal cause of unhappiness in the nation. He added, significantly, "most of us here present have been long working with minorities, and may have got into the habit of being dissatisfied." In the course of a long interview they discussed many aspects of the emancipation problem. The President made it clear that while he appreciated their interest and support, he alone was responsible for making decisions related to freedom and the war. Finally, he said, "All I can say now is that I believe the proclamation has knocked the bottom out of slavery, though at no time have I expected any sudden results from it."[9]

When the news of the Emancipation Proclamation reached Britain, a Cockney woman is reported to have run through the streets of London shouting, "Lincoln's been and gone and done it!" Her delight knew no limits, and it reflected the general reaction of the great mass of the British people. Lord Palmerston and Lord Russell could continue their flirtation with the rebellious states at their own peril. Their willingness to wink at the Confederacy's purchasing of ships from British builders was a scandal which the Union would not permit them to forget. But if they dared move closer to recognition of the Confederate government, they would discover that they would not have the support of their own constituents. The people of Britain, long devoted to the antislavery cause in many parts of the world, were fired to great excitement by the Emancipation Proclamation. "Mr. Lincoln's cause is just and holy, the cause of truth, and of universal humanity," wrote the well-to-do Birmingham merchant, Samuel A. Goddard.[10]

Most Britons did not express their feelings about the Proclamation by shouting in the London streets, as the Cockney woman did, or writing letters to the Birmingham *Post*, as Goddard did. But they made known their enthusiastic support of the Lincoln policy in a dozen different ways. As Henry Adams, writing from London, put it, the Proclamation was creating "an almost convulsive reaction in our favor all over this country." He chided the London *Times* for behaving like a "drunken drab," but he was certain that its hostility represented no substantial segment of the middle and lower classes. "Public opinion is deeply stirred here and finds expression in meetings, addresses to President Lincoln, deputations to us, standing committees to agitate the subject and to affect opinion, and all the other symptoms of a great popular movement peculiarly unpleasant to the upper classes here because it rests on the spontaneous action of the laboring classes and has a pestilous squint at sympathy with republicanism."[11]

Within a few weeks after the issuance of the Proclamation, some important public figures in Britain began to speak out in public—at first timidly, then more boldly—in support of the Northern policy. In late March, the Prime Minister, speaking in Edinburgh on the Civil War, expressed a feeling of horror of any war that brought in its wake so much suffering and bloodshed. This was the Palmerston style, to which the people had become accustomed. But this time there was a reply. On the following evening the Duke of Argyll said that when civil wars involved a high moral purpose, he for one was not ashamed of the ancient combination of the Bible and the sword. "Let it be enough for us to pray and hope that the contest, whenever it may be brought to an end, shall bring with it that great blessing to the white race which shall consist in the final freedom of the black."[12] Soon the British government became more respectful of what Argyll had called the combination of the Bible and the sword.

The broadening of the Union's war aims to include a crusade against slavery coincided with another important development. Serious grain shortages at home were forcing the British to look elsewhere for foodstuffs. The cotton supply was not yet acutely short, thanks to huge inventories at the beginning of the war, blockade-running during the war, and new sources of supply in India and Egypt. There were also new sources of grain supply, but the British had come to rely heavily on Northern wheat. Indeed, many thought it was indispensable. Perhaps, under the circumstances, the British government should not risk a rupture with the North, some leaders began to reason. As Her Majesty's Government began to look seriously at this problem, it also began to take cognizance of the pressures of the rank and file of the British people and the pressures of the Washington government. Hope for recognition of the Confederacy by Britain and the Continental powers faded away. The Emancipation Proclamation had played an important role in achieving this signal diplomatic victory.

In the months and years following January 1, 1863, Lincoln indicated in many ways that he fully appreciated the importance of the Emancipation Proclamation in the war effort. He knew that it could be an important factor in preventing European powers from moving closer to the Confederacy. He read with the greatest interest the reports from Charles Francis Adams about British reaction to the Proclamation. He even sought to influence British response to the Proclamation by suggesting the form that resolutions adopted in British meetings might take. The President wanted the people in Britain to adopt resolutions condemning any nation whose cornerstone was slavery. The proposed resolutions are so unique as an example of how a President sought to influence foreign public opinion and of the contempt that Lincoln had for slavery that they deserve extended quotation:

> Whereas, while heretofore, States, and Nations have tolerated slavery, recently, for the first in the world, an attempt has been made to construct a new Nation, upon the basis of, and with the primary, and fundamental object to maintain, enlarge, and perpetuate human slavery, therefore
>
> Resolved, That no such embryo State should ever be recognized by, or admitted into, the family of Christian and civilized nations; and that all ch/r/istian and civilized men everywhere should, by all lawful means, resist to the utmost, such recognition or admission.[13]

There is no record of these resolutions having been adopted at any of the numerous meetings in Britain. The fact remains, however, that many resolutions adopted in Britain contained sentiments similar to those expressed by Lincoln. Meanwhile, since the proposed resolutions were sent to Britain through Charles Sumner, it must have been comforting to the Massachusetts Senator and his colleagues to realize that the President's antislavery views in the resolution were about as rugged as theirs. Indeed, Sumner tried in vain to persuade the President to incorporate the substance of these views in his next annual message to Congress.

The President hoped that the Proclamation would be the instrument for the further prosecution of the war and the emancipation of slaves in states and parts of states excepted by the Proclamation. He followed with great interest the recruitment and activity of black troops that followed in the wake of emancipation. He noticed that the Confederates attacked black troops fiercely, and that was to be expected. "It is important to the enemy that such a force shall *not* take shape, and grow, and thrive, in the South; and in precisely the same proportion, it is important to us that it shall."[14] In

May the President said he would gladly receive "ten times ten thousand" black troops and would protect all who enlisted. On April 30, 1863, the Confederate Congress had decreed that black soldiers captured by the Confederate Army would be dealt with according to the laws of the state in which they were seized. The President found it necessary, therefore, to take steps to protect blacks in the armed services. On July 30 he issued an Executive Order of Retaliation that was sent out on the following day by the office of Adjutant General Lorenzo Thomas as General Orders No. 252. In the Order the President asserted that the law of nations and the uses and customs of war as carried on by civilized powers "permit no distinction as to color in the treatment of prisoners of war as public enemies." He notified the Confederates that if they sold or enslaved any persons because of color, they would have relapsed into barbarism and would be committing a crime against the civilization of the age. He warned that "for every soldier of the United States killed in violation of the laws of war, a rebel soldier shall be executed; and for every one enslaved by the enemy or sold into slavery, a rebel soldier shall be placed at hard labor on the public works. . . ."[15]

Lincoln had come to this decision reluctantly. A few weeks earlier Frederick Douglass, abolitionist turned recruiter, had visited the President and requested him to order equal pay and treatment for black troops and establish a policy of retaliation against the Confederacy for the mistreatment of black troops. Lincoln agreed with Douglass that blacks should receive equal pay and should be promoted when they deserved it, but he would have to wait until the nation became more accustomed to black soldiers. He said that he found it impossible to adopt a policy of retaliation that would punish the innocent for crimes committed by others.[16] The pressures and exigencies of the war were too much for Lincoln, and he issued the order regarding retaliation.

The Proclamation had officially launched the enlistment of blacks in the Army, and Lincoln was convinced that the service of black troops was so important that neither Confederates nor Unionists should obstruct their availability. He praised the conduct of blacks under fire and said that some of the generals who had been most successful in the field "believe the emancipation policy, and the use of colored troops, constitute the heaviest blow yet dealt to the rebellion; and that, at least one of those important successes, could not have been achieved when it was, but for the aid of black soldiers."[17] The President had no doubt of the loyalty of blacks to the Union, but he felt that their interest in their own freedom was an additional motive. This grew out of the government's emancipation policy, the wisdom of which Lincoln was even more certain before the end of the year.

Although the Proclamation did not apply to the border slave states—Missouri, Kentucky, Maryland, and Delaware—Lincoln hoped that it would be a stimulus for the development of emancipation policies in those areas. He was pleased to learn in the spring of 1863 that the state of Missouri was considering a plan for gradual emancipation. When the state officials inquired if the federal government would protect the people of Missouri in their slave property between the time of the repeal of the slave provisions of the constitution and the enactment of an emancipation plan, Lincoln said the government would provide such protection. He made it clear that it would be given only on a temporary basis and not "beyond what can be fairly claimed under the constitution." He assured them that the military force would not be used to subvert the temporarily reserved legal rights in slaves during the progress of emancipation.[18] He very much regretted that the beginning of emancipation was postponed for seven years. This could hardly be regarded as temporary, and he made clear his displeasure.

Despite the fact that the immediate results of the Emancipation Proclamation were not always measurable, Lincoln was pleased with what he had done. Over and over again he expressed the view that he had done the right thing. It had not had an adverse effect on the course of the war. The war, he told a correspondent in the summer of 1863, had "certainly progressed as favorably for us, since the issue of the proclamation as before." The Proclamation was valid, and he would never retract it. Moreover, it reflected his own repugnance to slavery. As an antislavery man, he wrote Major General Nathaniel P. Banks, he had a motive for issuing the Proclamation that went beyond military considerations. At last he had been able to strike the blow for freedom that he had long wanted to do.

Finally, Lincoln hoped that the Proclamation would provide the basis for a new attitude and policy for blacks. That all slaves would soon be free was a reality that all whites should face. "Those who shall have tasted actual freedom I believe can never be slaves, or quasi slaves again." He hoped, therefore, that the several states would adopt some practical system "by which the two races could gradually live themselves out of their old relation to each other, and both come out better prepared for the new." He hoped that states would provide for the education of blacks, and he went so far as to suggest to Governor Michael Hahn of Louisiana that his state might consider extending the franchise to free blacks of education and property.[19]

Thus, in many ways the Proclamation affected the course of the war as well as Lincoln's way of thinking about the problem of blacks in the United States. Abroad, it rallied large numbers of people to the North's side and became a valuable instrument of American foreign policy. At home it sharpened the issues of the war and provided a moral and humanitarian ingredient that had been lacking. It fired the leaders with a new purpose and gave to the President a new weapon. Small wonder that he no longer promoted the idea of colonization. Small wonder that he began to advocate education and the franchise for blacks. They were a new source of strength that deserved to be treated as the loyal citizens that they were.

For the last one hundred and thirty-two years the Emancipation Proclamation has maintained its place as one of America's truly important documents. Even when the principles it espoused were not universally endorsed and even when its beneficiaries were the special target of mistreatment of one kind or another, the Proclamation somehow retained its hold on the very people who saw its promises unfulfilled. It did not do this because of the perfection of the goal to which it aspired. At best it sought to save the Union by freeing *some* of the slaves. Nor did it do it by the sublimity of its language. It had neither the felicity of the Declaration of Independence nor the simple grandeur of the Gettysburg Address. But in a very real sense it was another step toward the extension of the ideal of equality about which Jefferson had written.

Lincoln wrote the Emancipation Proclamation amid severe psychological and legal handicaps. Unlike Jefferson, whose Declaration of Independence was a clean break with a legal and constitutional system that had hitherto restricted thought and action, Lincoln was compelled to forge a document of freedom for the slaves within the existing constitutional system and in a manner that would give even greater support to that constitutional system. This required not only courage and daring but considerable ingenuity as well. As in so many of Lincoln's acts the total significance and validity of the measure were not immediately apparent, even among those who were sympathetic with its aims. Gradually, the greatness of the document dawned upon the nation and the world. Gradually, it took its place with the great documents of human freedom.

When English America was settled in the seventeenth century it soon became the haven for people who were religiously and socially discontent, economically disadvantaged, and politically disoriented. It was not until they

broke away from the mother country that they began effectively to realize the existence of which they had dreamed.
The break was so complete and the ideology of the break so
far-reaching that the only valid base on which to build the
New World republic was one characterized by democracy
and equality. The tragedy of this republic was that as long as
human slavery existed its base had a fallacy that made it
both incongruous and specious. The great value of the
Emancipation Proclamation was that in its first century
it provided the base with a reinforcement that made it at
long last valid and worthy. Perhaps in its second century it
would give real meaning and purpose to the Declaration of
Independence.

End of Unrequited Toil

M arch 4, 1865, was a dark, dreary, gusty day in the nation's capital, but the future of the nation seemed bright. Arkansas, Louisiana, Maryland, and Missouri had abolished slavery by act of their legislatures. Congress had passed the resolution that, before the end of the year, was to become the Thirteenth Amendment. The President still favored compensation to the owners of emancipated slaves, but the hearing he received from his Cabinet in 1865 was no more sympathetic than the one he received in 1862. The Confederate armies were in flight, and the end of the war was in sight.

As the inaugural party took its place on the Capitol portico, the assembled throng could see the complete dome with the bronze statue of Freedom at long last adorning it. Meanwhile, the President and his party could look out on a crowd that was the most unique that had ever attended the inauguration of an American President. There were not only white Americans but black Americans—free black Americans—as well. It was a moving sight, the significance of which was not lost on President Lincoln. Looking out over the crowd, he caught the eye of the distinguished black leader, Frederick Douglass, whom he greeted warmly.

They were to greet each other again later in the day at the White House reception.

The entire occasion was "wonderfully quiet, earnest, and solemn." After the President took his oath of office for his second term, he delivered his brief address. With the end of the war and of slavery clearly in sight, he said,

> *Fondly do we hope, fervently do we pray, that this mighty scourge of war may speedily pass away. Yet, if God wills that it continue until all the wealth piled by the bondsman's two hundred and fifty years of unrequited toil shall be sunk, and until every drop of blood drawn with the lash shall be paid by another drawn with the sword, as was said three thousand years ago, so still it must be said, "The judgments of the Lord are true and righteous altogether."*

Sources

I n view of the fact that the text of this work has been ex-
tensively documented, it does not seem necessary to
provide a definitive bibliography, source by source. Instead,
it would seem to be more desirable to indicate here some of
the more important sources for one who would seek further
information and discussion about the Emancipation Proclamation. Most of these sources have been cited; some have
not. All have been extremely valuable in any treatment of
the Emancipation Proclamation.

The three different drafts of the Emancipation Proclamation are in three different places. The draft of July 22,
1862, is in the Library of Congress; that of September 22,
1862, is in the New York State Library; and the photographic reproduction of the draft of January 1, 1863, is in
the National Archives. The most important source of official
Washington is, of course, Abraham Lincoln. The edition of
his *Collected Works*, edited by Roy Basler in seven volumes
(New Brunswick, 1953) is by far the most satisfactory. Two
members of Lincoln's Cabinet have left extensive diaries
and autobiographical materials that are most helpful. They
are the Chase papers in the Library of Congress and his
diaries, *Inside Lincoln's Cabinet: The Civil War Diaries of*

Salmon P. Chase, edited by David Donald (New York, 1954) and the first volume of the *Diary of Gideon Welles* (Boston, 1911). One of Lincoln's secretaries kept a valuable account of the President's activities and problems that may be consulted in *Lincoln and the Civil War in the Diaries and Letters of John Hay*, edited by Tyler Dennett (New York, 1939).

The actions of Congress as well as the statements of many of its members on the Proclamation may be followed in the *Congressional Globe* and the *Congressional Record*. Of the individual members who have left important records of their own activities *The Diary of Orville H. Browning* (Springfield, 1925) and *The Works of Charles Sumner*, volumes six and seven (Boston, 1872 and 1873) are outstanding. In the Confederacy the *Journal of the Congress of the Confederate States of America*, seven volumes (Washington, 1904–1905) and *A Compilation of the Messages and Papers of the Confederacy*, edited by J. D. Richardson in two volumes (Nashville, 1906) provide the significant primary source materials of that government. For the Confederacy and the Union important supplementary sources are the *American Annual Cyclopedia and Register of Important Events of the Year 1863* (New York, 1864), and Frank Moore's *Rebellion Record*, eleven volumes (New York, 1868). The monumental *The War of the Rebellion: A Compilation of the Official Records of the Union and Confederate Armies*, 127 volumes (Washington, 1880–1901) should not be overlooked.

Contemporary accounts by a variety of persons provide relevant and valuable commentaries and sidelights on the Proclamation. Among them are Noah Brooks, *Washington in Lincoln's Time,* edited by Herbert Mitgang (New York, 1958); F. B. Carpenter, *The Inner Life of Abraham Lincoln: Six Months at the White House* (New York, 1869); William O. Stoddard, *Inside the White House in War Time* (New York, 1890); Frederick Douglass, *The Life and Times of Frederick Douglass* (New York, 1938); Henry M. Turner, *The Negro in Slavery, War, and Peace* (Philadelphia, 1913);

Moncure D. Conway, *Autobiography: Memories and Experiences*, two volumes (Boston 1904); and W. W. Patton, *President Lincoln and the Chicago Memorial on Emancipation* (Baltimore, 1888). Another group of contemporaries commented specifically on the significance and impact of the Proclamation. Their works are *The Journal of Charlotte Forten*, edited by Ray A. Billington (New York, 1953); Thomas W. Higginson, *Army Life in a Black Regiment*, edited by John Hope Franklin (Boston, 1962); James C. Welling, *Addresses, Lectures, and Other Papers* (Cambridge, 1903); Benjamin P. Curtis, *Executive Power* (Boston, 1862); Charles P. Kirkland, *A Letter to . . . Benjamin Curtis in Review of His Recently Published Pamphlet on the "Emancipation Proclamation"* (New York, 1862); and William H. Herndon, *History and Personal Recollections of Abraham Lincoln* (Springfield, Ill., no date).

The newspapers and magazines of the period were all sensitive to the importance of the Proclamation. Some, however, deserve special mention as being representative of the prevailing views of the period. In Washington the *National Intelligencer,* the *Bee*, and the *Evening Star* are most valuable. Among the Northern papers and magazines, those in New York, the *Times, World, Age,* and *Tribune*; in New England, the Boston *Evening Transcript*, the *Liberator*, and the Providence *Journal*; and in the Midwest, the Cincinnati *Daily Gazette* give a fair cross section of press opinion. *Harper's Weekly* and *Atlantic* provide excellent magazine source material. In the South the Richmond *Examiner,* Charleston *Mercury*, the New Orleans *Daily Picayune*, and the Arkansas *State Gazette* will give an adequate picture. Britain's best newspaper and magazine sources for this study were the London *Times*, Manchester *Guardian, The Economist*, and the *Spectator*. On the Continent, *Le Constitutionnel* and *Il Giornale di Roma* are representative.

One of the best sources of information on the impact of the Proclamation abroad is the reports of the United States representatives abroad. In the National Archives are the dispatches from these representatives filed with the Department of State. There are also the Papers on Foreign Affairs Presented to Congress, commonly known as "Diplomatic Correspondence" and published annually during this period. In this connection one should read *A Cycle of Adams Letters, 1861–1865*, edited by Worthington Chauncey Ford, two volumes (Boston, 1920); Samuel A. Goddard, *The American Rebellion: Letters on the American Rebellion* (London, 1870); Karl Marx and Friedrich Engels, *The Civil War in the United States* (New York, 1937); and Emile Norvette-Delorme, *Les États-Unis et l'Europe; rupture de l'Union, reconnaisance due Sud, abolition de l'esclavage* (Paris, 1863).

Many secondary works have given attention to various aspects of the history of the Proclamation. Among the very few that deal with it exclusively are Henry Steele Commager, *The Great Proclamation, A Book for Young Americans* (Indianapolis, 1960); Charles Eberstadt, "Lincoln's Emancipation Proclamation," *The New Colophon* (1950), 312–56; and Victor Rosewater, "Lincoln in Emancipation Days," *St. Nicholas*, LXIV (February 1937), 12–13, 47. Among the most valuable biographies are J. C. Nicolay and John Hay, *Abraham Lincoln, A History,* ten volumes (New York, 1890); Carl Sandburg, *Abraham Lincoln, The War Years,* four volumes (New York, 1939); Benjamin P. Thomas, *Abraham Lincoln* (New York, 1952); Reinhard Luthin, *The Real Abraham Lincoln* (Englewood Cliffs, 1960); and various studies of Lincoln by James G. Randall. Allan Nevins's monumental history of the Civil War period covers numerous relevant problems related to the Emancipation Proclamation. Especially valuable is his *The War for the Union: The War Becomes Revolution, 1862–1863* (New York, 1960).

Among the important lives of contemporaries are Charles E. Hamlin, *The Life and Times of Hannibal Hamlin* (Cambridge, 1899); William Dudley Foulke, *Life of Oliver P. Morton* (Indianapolis, 1899); William C. Harris, *The Public Life of Zachariah Chandler, 1851–1875* (Chicago, 1917);

Henry G. Pearson, *The Life of John A. Andrew* (Boston, 1904); Robert B. Warden, *An Account of the Private Life and Public Services of Salmon Portland Chase* (Cincinnati, 1874); Benjamin Quarles, *Frederick Douglass* (Washington, 1948); and Benjamin Thomas and Harold Hyman, *Stanton: The Life and Times of Lincoln's Secretary of War* (New York, 1962). The best account of the writing of the first draft of the Proclamation is David Homer Bates, *Lincoln in the Telegraph Office: Recollections of the United States Military Corps During the Civil War* (New York, 1907). The impact of the Proclamation on political developments may be followed in Wood Gray, *The Hidden Civil War* (New York, 1942); Sidney Brummer, *Political History of New York During the Period of the Civil War* (New York, 1911); Arthur C. Cole, *The Era of the Civil War* (Illinois) (Springfield, 1919); Kenneth Stampp, *Indiana Politics During the Civil War* (Indianapolis, 1949); George H. Porter, *Ohio Politics During the Civil War Period* (New York, 1911); and William B. Hesseltine, *Lincoln and the War Governors* (New York, 1948). See also, William B. Hesseltine and Hazel C. Wolf, "The Altoona Conference and the Emancipation Proclamation," *Pennsylvania Magazine of History and Biography, LXXI* (July 1947), pp. 195–205.

Margaret Leech's *Reveille in Washington* (New York, 1941) is the best secondary account of life in the capital during the Civil War. Benjamin Quarles's two books that are indispensable for an understanding of blacks during the period are *The Negro and the Civil War* (Boston, 1954) and *Lincoln and the Negro* (New York, 1962). Bell I. Wiley's *Southern Negroes, 1861–1865* (New York, 1953), *Life of Johnny Reb,* and *Life of Billy Yank* (Indianapolis, 1943 and 1951) are extremely useful. Other important sources on blacks are John Hope Franklin, *From Slavery to Freedom: A History of American Negroes* (New York, 1956); W. E. B. Du Bois, *Black Reconstruction* (New York, 1935); Herbert Aptheker, *A Documentary History of the People in the United States* (New York, 1951); John E. Washington, *They Knew Lincoln* (New York, 1942); Dudley T. Cornish, *The*

Sable Arm: Negro Troops in the Union Army, 1861–1865 (New York, 1956); Charles H. Wesley, "Lincoln's Plan for Colonizing the Emancipated Negro," *Journal of Negro History*, IV (January 1919), 7–21; and Harvey Wish, "Slave Disloyalty under the Confederacy," *Journal of Negro History*, XXIII (October 1938), 435–50.

There are many histories of the Confederacy. Among the best known and most important are Clement Eaton, *A History of the Southern Confederacy* (New York, 1956); Charles P. Roland, *The Confederacy* (Chicago, 1960); and E. Merton Coulter, *The Confederate States of America* (Baton Rouge, 1950). One should also consult Rembert W. Patrick, *Jefferson Davis and His Cabinet* (Baton Rouge, 1944) and Dunbar Rowland, *Jefferson Davis, Constitutionalist*, ten volumes (Jackson, 1923).

Perhaps the most important work dealing with the impact of the Proclamation abroad is E. D. Adams, *Great Britain and the American Civil War*, two volumes (New York, 1958). But many other works have dealt with the matter. Among the more significant are Helen McDonald, *Canadian Public Opinion of the American Civil War* (New York, 1926); Robin Winks, *Canada and the United States: The Civil War Years* (Baltimore, 1960); and Frank Owsley, *King Cotton Diplomacy* (Chicago, 1959).

There have been several surveys of European public opinion during the Civil War. Those containing material on the Emancipation Proclamation are Donaldson Jordan and Edwin J. Pratt, *Europe and the American Civil War* (Boston, 1931); Belle B. Sideman and Lillian Friedman, *Europe Looks at the Civil War* (New York, 1960); and W. Reed West, *Contemporary French Opinion of the Civil War* (Baltimore, 1924). Of the numerous works bearing on Russia and the Proclamation, see Albert A. Woldman, *Lincoln and the Russians* (New York, 1952) and Wharton Barton, "The Secret of Russia's Friendship," *Independent*, LVI (March 24, 1904), 645–49.

Notes

PROLOGUE

1. Salmon P. Chase, *Inside Lincoln's Cabinet: The Civil War Diaries of Salmon P. Chase*, edited by David Donald, New York, 1954, pp. 149–50.

1

1. Eric Williams, *Capitalism and Slavery*. Chapel Hill, 1944, p. 45. Cowper had made the statement in "The Task," written in 1783.
2. Marion Lansing, *Liberators and Heroes of Mexico and Central America*. Boston, 1941, p. 103.
3. Alfred B. Thomas, *Latin America: A History*. New York, 1956, pp. 236, 590.
4. For a succinct discussion of the condition of slaves in the Americas at the time of freedom, see Frank Tannenbaum, *Slave and Citizen, The Negro in the Americas*. New York, 1947, pp. 103–16.
5. John Hope Franklin, *From Slavery to Freedom: A History of American Negroes*. New York, 1956, p. 342.
6. For a discussion of the American reaction to developments in Haiti, see Dwight L. Dumond, *Anti-Slavery: The Crusade for Freedom in America*. Ann Arbor, 1961, pp. 112–14.
7. Quoted from *The West Indian* on the cover of *The American Anti-Slavery Almanac for 1839*. New York, 1839.
8. Nicholas V. Riasanovsky, *Russia and the West in the Teaching of the Slavophiles: A Study of Romantic Ideology*. Cambridge, 1952, pp. 136–37.

9. Jesse D. Clarkson, *A History of Russia*. New York, 1961, pp. 276–80.

10. Paul Milyoukov, *Russia and Its Crisis*. Chicago, 1906, p. 266.

11. Clarkson, op. cit., pp. 299–301.

12. Albert A. Woldman, *Lincoln and the Russians*. New York, 1952, p. 172. See also Max Laserson, *The American Impact on Russia—Diplomatic and Ideological—1784–1917*. New York, 1950, pp. 187–88.

13. Carl Becker, *The Declaration of Independence, A Study in the History of Political Ideas*. New York, 1953, pp. 212–13.

14. Roy P. Basler, ed., *The Collected Works of Abraham Lincoln*. New Brunswick, 1953, vol IV, p. 263.

15. Ibid., vol. V, p. 222.

16. *U.S. Statutes*, XII, 319.

17. New York *Times*, August 7, 1861.

18. *Congressional Globe*, 37th Congress, Second Session, pp. 348, 355–56.

19. *Annual Cyclopedia for 1862*, pp. 333–44.

20. Benjamin A. Quarles, *Lincoln and the Negro*. New York, 1962, p. 104.

21. *Collected Works*, vol. V, p. 192.

22. Henry G. Pearson, *James S. Wadsworth of Genesco*. New York, 1913.

23. *U.S. Statutes*, XII, 432.

24. On July 12 he issued an appeal to border state Representatives in Congress to support his program of compensated emancipation. *Collected Works*, vol. V, p. 317.

25. *Collected Works*. vol. V, pp. 328–31.

26. *U.S. Statutes*, XII, 591.

27. *Collected Works*, vol. V, pp. 29–31.

28. Ibid., p. 48 ff.

29. Ibid., pp. 144, 160.

30. *The Works of Charles Sumner*. Boston, 1872, vol. VI, p. 31.

31. Sumner to Andrew, December 27, 1871, in Sumner, *Works*, vol. VI, p. 152.

32. Ibid., vol VII, pp. 214–15.

33. *Douglass' Monthly*, May 1861.

34. New York *Times*, February 13, 1862.

35. *Collected Works*, vol. V, pp. 278–79.

36. Ibid., p. 327.

37. New York *Tribune*, August 20, 1862.

38. *Collected Works*, vol. V, pp. 388–89.

39. New York *Tribune*, August 25, 1862.

40. *Collected Works*, vol. V, pp. 419–25.

2

1. William H. Herndon, *History and Personal Recollections of Abraham Lincoln*. Springfield, n.d., p. 76.
2. Emanuel Hertz, *Abraham Lincoln*. New York, 1931, vol. II, p. 531.
3. Lincoln to Albert G. Hodges, Frankfort, Kentucky, April 4, 1864, *Collected Works*, vol. VII, p. 281.
4. Lincoln, *Collected Works*, vol. V, p. 371.
5. Ibid., vol. VII, p. 282.
6. F. B. Carpenter, *The Inner Life of Abraham Lincoln: Six Months at the White House*. New York, 1869, pp. 20–21.
7. David H. Bates, *Lincoln at the Telegraph Office*. New York, 1907, pp. 138–41.
8. Lincoln, *Collected Works*, vol. V, pp. 275–76.
9. Charles E. Hamlin, *The Life and Times of Hannibal Hamlin*. Cambridge, 1899, pp. 428–29.
10. Gideon Welles, *Diary*. Boston, 1911, vol. I, pp. 70–71.
11. Lincoln, *Collected Works*, vol. V, pp. 336–37.
12. Carpenter, op. cit., p. 20.
13. Benjamin Thomas and Harold Hyman, *Stanton: The Life and Times of Lincoln's Secretary of War*. New York, 1962, p. 239.
14. David Donald, ed., *Inside Lincoln's Cabinet: The Civil War Diaries of Salmon P. Chase*. New York, 1954, pp. 97–98.
15. Ibid., pp. 105–106.
16. Tyler Dennett, ed., *Lincoln and the Civil War in the Diaries and Letters of John Hay*. New York, 1939, p. 50.
17. Welles, op. cit., vol. I, pp. 142–43.
18. Joseph Emery to Chase, September 29, 1862, Ms. in the Chase Papers, Library of Congress.
19. John Livingston to Chase, October 1, 1862, Ms. in the Chase Papers, Library of Congress.

3

1. Charles Eberstadt, "Lincoln's Emancipation Proclamation," *The New Colophon*, 1950, pp. 317–18.
2. Washington *Evening Star*, September 24, 1862.
3. Lincoln, *Collected Works*, vol. V. p. 441.
4. New York *Tribune*, September 29, 1862.
5. New York *Times*, October 23, 1862.
6. New York *Tribune*, October 13, 1862.
7. Ibid., October 7, 1862.
8. Benjamin Quarles, *Frederick Douglass*. Washington, 1948, p. 198.
9. *National Republican*, September 23, 1862.

10. New York *Tribune*, September 23 and 24, 1862.

11. New York *Times*, September 23, 1862.

12. Boston *Evening Transcript*, September 23 and 24, 1862.

13. Providence *Journal*, September 24, 1862.

14. Cincinnati *Daily Gazette*, September 23, 1862.

15. *Harper's Weekly*, October 4, 1862.

16. Lincoln, *Collected Works*, vol. V, p. 444.

17. Allen T. Rice, *Reminiscences of Abraham Lincoln by Distinguished Men of His Time*. New York, 1888, pp. 532–33. Stanly revealed to James C. Welling of the *National Intelligencer* his discussion with Lincoln.

18. Washington *Evening Star*, September 24, 1862.

19. *National Intelligencer*, September 23 and 24, 1862.

20. New York *Herald*, September 24, 1862.

21. Baltimore *American*, September 24, 1862.

22. Quoted in the *Providence Journal*, September 25, 1862.

23. Newburyport *Herald*, September 26, 1862.

24. Quoted in the *Daily Richmond Examiner,* October 16, 1862.

25. New York *World*, September 24, 1862.

26. Richmond *Examiner*, September 29, 1862.

27. Richmond *Whig*, September 29, 1862.

28. Richmond *Enquirer*, September 30, 1862.

29. Charleston *Mercury*, October 1, 1862.

30. Arkansas *State Gazette*, October 11, 1862.

31. Richmond *Whig*, October 3, 1862; New Orleans *Picayune*, October 11, 1862; Richmond *Examiner*, September 29 and October 16, 1862.

32. Richmond *Enquirer,* October 1, 1862.

33. Charleston *Mercury*, October 1, 1862.

34. Arkansas *State Gazette*, October 11, 1862.

35. Fred Landon, "Canadian Opinion of Abraham Lincoln," *Dalhousie Review*, II (October 1922), 332.

36. Toronto *Globe*, September 23, 1862, quoted in Helen G. MacDonald, *Canadian Public Opinion of the American Civil War*. New York, 1926, p. 102.

37. Robin W. Winks, *Canada and the United States: The Civil War Years*. Baltimore, 1960, p. 129.

38. Toronto *Leader*, October 25, 1862, quoted in MacDonald, op. cit., p. 102.

39. Martin B. Duberman, *Charles Francis Adams, 1807–1886*. Boston, 1961, pp. 298–99.

40. *Punch*, XL (March 30, 1861), 134.

41. London *Times*, October 9, 1862.

42. London *Post*, October 8, 1862.

43. Henry Sanford to W. H. Seward (Private), October 15, 1862, Dispatches from U.S. Ministers to Belgium, Ms. in the National Archives.

44. Diplomatic Dispatches from United States Ministers to Great Britain, Microcopy 30, Roll 77.

45. Quoted in Ephraim D. Adams, *Great Britain and the American Civil War*. New York, 1958, vol. II, p. 101.

46. Manchester *Guardian*, October 7 and October 13, 1862.

47. *Spectator*, XXXV (October 11, 1862), 1125–26.

48. London *Times*, October 6 and October 7, 1862.

49. *The Economist*, XX (October 25, 1862), 1177–78.

50. *Saturday Review*, XIV (October 11, 1862), 425–26.

51. "Address of the Inhabitants of Birmingham to His Excellency Abraham Lincoln," n.d., Ms. in the National Archives.

52. Address to President Lincoln by the Working-Men of Manchester, England, December 31, 1862, quoted in Henry Steele Commager, *Documents of American History*, New York, 1958, p. 418.

53. London *Star*, October 6, 1862, quoted in the New York *Times*, October 22, 1862.

54. Frank L. Owsley, *King Cotton Diplomacy*. Chicago, 1939, p. 332.

55. William L. Dayton to W. H. Seward, October 25, 1862, Dispatches from U.S. Ministers to France, Ms. in the National Archives.

56. *Le Constitutionnel*, October 8, 1862.

57. Quoted in the New York *Times*, October 27, 1862.

58. W. Reed West, *Contemporary French Opinion of the American Civil War*. Baltimore, 1924, p. 85.

59. New York *Times*, October 27, 1862.

60. Sanford to Seward, October 30, 1862, Dispatches from U.S. Ministers to Belgium, Ms. in the National Archives.

61. *Journal des Débats*, October 29, 1862.

62. Quoted in the New York *Times*, October 27, 1862.

63. Sanford to Seward, October 8, 1862, Dispatches from U.S. Ministers to Belgium, Ms. in the National Archives.

64. Horatio J. Perry to W. H. Seward, October 25, 1862, Dispatches from U.S. Ministers to Spain, Ms. in the National Archives.

65. Gustavus Koener to W. H. Seward, October 13, 1862, Dispatches from U.S. Ministers to Spain, Ms. in the National Archives.

66. Stoeckl to Foreign Office, September 25, 1862, Dispatches of Russian Representatives to U.S. to Home Government, copy in the Library of Congress. See also Albert A. Woldman, *Lincoln and the Russians.* New York, 1952, p. 182.

67. Bayard Taylor to W. H. Seward, October 29, 1862, Department of State, Diplomatic Dispatches, Russian, Microfilm 35, Roll 19.

68. Belle B. Sideman and Lillian Friedman, eds., *Europe Looks at the Civil War*. New York, 1860, pp. 196–97.
69. Taylor to Seward, December 17, 1862.
70. *Official Records of the Rebellion*, Series III, vol. II, pp. 584–85.
71. Kenneth M. Stampp, *Indiana Politics During the Civil War*. Indianapolis, 1949, p. 163.
72. *Official Records*, Series I, vol. XIX, pt. 2, p. 395.
73. Quoted in J. Cutler Andrews, *The North Reports the Civil War*. Pittsburgh, 1955, pp. 315–16.
74. *Official Records*, Series I, vol. LII, pp. 358–61.
75. W. E. B. Du Bois, *Black Reconstruction*, New York, 1935, pp. 55–83; and Bell I. Wiley, *Southern Negroes, 1861–1865*, New York, 1953, pp. 175–90.
76. New York *Times*, September 29, 1862.
77. Benjamin Quarles, *The Negro in the Civil War*. Boston, 1953, p. 165.
78. Pearson, *Wadsworth*, p. 156.
79. Sidney Brummer, *Political History of New York during the Period of the Civil War*. New York, 1911, 249–51.
80. William B. Hesseltine, *Lincoln and the War Governors*, New York, 1948, p. 266; and Henry G. Pearson, *The Life of John A. Andrew*, Boston, 1904, vol. II, p. 51.
81. George H. Porter, *Ohio Politics During the Civil War Period*. New York, 1911, p. 105.
82. Eugene H. Roseboom, *The Civil War Era*. Columbus, 1944, pp. 401–402.
83. Kenneth Stampp, *Indiana Politics During the Civil War*, Indianapolis, 1949, pp. 147–48; and William D. Foulke, *Life of Oliver P. Morton*, Indianapolis, 1899, vol. I, p. 207.
84. Arthur C. Cole, *Era of the Civil War*. Springfield, 1919, p. 300.
85. John Hay to J. G. Nicolay, October 28, 1862, in Dennett, op. cit., p. 52.
86. Wilmer C. Harris, *Public Life of Zachariah Chandler, 1851–1875*, Chicago, 1917, p. 67; and Hesseltine, op. cit., pp. 267–68.
87. There is an excellent discussion of the election in Allan Nevins, *The War for the Union: War Becomes Revolution, 1862–1863*. New York, 1960, pp. 299–322.
88. Lincoln to Carl Schurz, November 10, 1862. *Collected Works*, vol. V, pp. 493–95.
89. Marx to Engels, November 15, 1862, in Karl Marx and Friedrich Engels, *The Civil War in the United States*. New York, 1937, p. 260.
90. Lincoln, *Collected Works*, vol. V, pp. 518–37.
91. These debates are in the *Congressional Globe*, Thirty-seventh Congress, Third Session, pp. 15–151 and Appendix, pp. 40–44.

92. New York *Tribune*, November 24, 1862, quoted in Lincoln, *Collected Works*, vol. V, pp. 503–504.

93. Benjamin P. Curtis, *Executive Power*. Boston, 1862.

94. Charles P. Kirkland, *A Letter to the Honorable Benjamin P. Curtis... in Review of His Recently Published Pamphlet on the "Emancipation Proclamation."* New York, 1862.

95. Lincoln, *Collected Works*, vol. V, p. 544.

96. Ibid., vol. V, pp. 544–45.

97. See Nevins, op. cit., pp. 343–68.

98. "The Emancipation Pen," *Proceedings of the Massachusetts Historical Society*, XLIV (1910–1911), p. 596.

99. Oliver H. Browning, *Diary*. Springfield, 1925, vol. I, p. 606.

100. Welles, *Diary*, vol. I, p. 209.

101. Lincoln, *Collected Works*, vol. VI, p. 25.

102. Welles, *Diary*, vol. I, p. 210.

103. Chase's complete communication to the President, dated December 31, 1862, is in Robert B. Warden, *An Account of the Private Life and Public Services of Salmon Portland Chase*. Cincinnati, 1874, pp. 513–15.

104. Washington *Evening Star*, January 1, 1863.

105. New York *Times*, January 1, 1863.

4

1. Eberstadt, loc. cit., p. 322.

2. John G. Nicolay and John Hay, *Abraham Lincoln, A History*. New York, 1914, vol. VI, 429.

3. Carpenter, op. cit., p. 21.

4. Eberstadt, loc. cit., pp. 321–23.

5. New York *Times*, January 1, 1863.

6. Victor Rosewater, "Lincoln in Emancipation Days," *St. Nicholas*, LXIV (February 1937), p. 12.

7. Washington *Evening Star*, January 2, 1863.

8. Henry M. Turner, *The Negro in Slavery, War, and Peace*, Philadelphia, 1913, pp. 6–7; and Quarles, *Lincoln and the Negro*, p. 142.

9. New York *Times*, January 6, 1863.

10. Ibid., January 6, 1863.

11. Ibid., January 6, 1863.

12. Ralph Waldo Emerson, *Poems*. Boston 1892, pp. 174–77.

13. The *Liberator*, January 9, 1863.

14. Frederick Douglass, *Life and Times of Frederick Douglass*. New York, 1941, p. 389.

15. The *Liberator*, January 9, 1863.

16. New York *Times*, January 4, 1863.

17. New York *Times*, February 4, 1863.

18. Ray Allen Billington, ed., *The Journal of Charlotte Forten*. New York, 1953, p. 153.

19. Thomas Wentworth Higginson, *Army Life in A Black Regiment*, edited by John Hope Franklin. Boston, 1962, pp. 39–41.

20. Billington, op. cit., p. 157.

21. *National Republican*, January 1 and 2, 1863.

22. Washington *Daily Morning Chronicle*, January 2, 1863.

23. New York *Daily Tribune*, January 3, 1863.

24. New York *Times*, January 3, 1863.

25. Cincinnati *Daily Gazette*, January 3, 1863.

26. Washington *National Intelligencer*, January 3, 1863.

27. New York *World*, January 1 and 3, 1863.

28. New York *Herald*, January 3, 1863.

29. Quoted in the *Liberator,* January 9, 1863.

30. Lincoln, *Collected Works*, vol. VI, p. 48.

31. *Congressional Globe*, 37th Congress, 3rd Session, Appendix, pp. 45, 161.

32. New York *Herald*, January 8, 1863; and Washington *National Intelligencer*, January 10, 1863.

33. Wendell Phillips, *Speeches, Lectures, and Letters*, Boston, 1894, vol. I, p. 530.

34. Richmond *Examiner,* January 7, 1863.

35. Richmond *Whig*, January 7, 1863.

36. Augusta *Chronicle and Sentinel*, January 9, 1863. See also the Nashville *Dispatch*, January 6, 1863.

37. Dunbar Rowland, *Jefferson Davis, Constitutionalist: His Letters, Papers and Speeches*. Jackson, 1923, vol. 5, pp. 409–11.

38. See New York *Times*, January 1, 1863.

39. Bell I. Wiley, *The Life of Billy Yank: The Common Soldier of the Union*. Indianapolis, 1952, pp. 41–42.

40. Booker T. Washington, *Up from Slavery*. New York, 1959, p. 5.

41. Elizabeth Bryant Johnston, *Christmas in Kentucky, 1862*. Washington, 1892, pp. 12–14.

42. Wiley, *Southern Negroes*, pp. 66–67.

43. Ibid., p. 83.

44. See John Hope Franklin, *The Civil War Diary of James T. Ayers*. Springfield, 1947.

45. London *Times*, January 15, 1863.

46. *Saturday Review*, XV (January 17 and 24, 1863), 68, 98.

47. *Spectator,* XXXVI (January 17, 1863), 1520.

48. John Ruskin to Charles Eliot Norton, February 10, 1863, in Sideman, op. cit., p. 218.

49. Earl Russell to Lord Lyons, January 17, 1863. *Parliamentary Papers*, LXXII (1863), no. 1, 51–52.

50. Adams, *Britain and the Civil War*, vol. II, p. 107.

51. Richard Cobden to Charles Sumner, February 13, 1863, in Sideman, loc. cit., p. 221–22. See also Henry Sanford to Seward, February 23, 1863, Dispatches of U.S. Ministers to Belgium, Ms. in the National Archives.

52. Henry Adams to Charles F. Adams, Jr., January 30, 1863, in Worthington C. Ford, editor, *A Cycle of Adams Letters, 1861–1865*. Boston, 1920, vol. I, p. 243.

53. Copies of all the resolutions mentioned are in *Diplomatic Correspondence*, 1863, pp. 54, 56, 105, 111, 123, 134–35.

54. Adams to Seward, March 5, 1863, Department of State, Diplomatic Dispatches, Microfilm 30, Roll 78.

55. Lyons to Russell, March 10, 1863, in Adams, *Britain and the Civil War*, vol. II, p. 14.

56. Sanford to Adams, January 16, 1862, Dispatches of U.S. Ministers to Belgium, Ms. in the National Archives.

57. J. W. Schulte Nordholt, "The Civil War Letters of the Dutch Ambassador," *Journal of the Illinois State Historical Society*, LIV (Winter, 1861), 363–64 and in conversations with the author of the article.

58. Jordan and Pratt, op. cit., p. 220.

59. Sideman, op. cit., pp. 219–20.

60. Koener to Seward, January 24, 1863, Dispatches of United States Ministers to Spain, Ms. in the National Archives.

61. Jordan and Pratt, op. cit., pp. 249–53.

62. Pius IX, Pontificus Maximi, *Acta*, (Roma, 1864), vol. III, pp. 530–532 (Biblioteca Vaticana). See also *Osservatore Romano*, January 24, 1863.

63. Massimo d'Azeglio, *I Miei Ricordi*. Firenze, 1876, vol. I, pp. 57–58.

64. *Il Giornale di Roma*, January 7, 1863.

65. Woldman, op. cit., p. 182.

66. Taylor to Seward, January 27, 1863, Department of State Diplomatic Dispatches, Russia, Microfilm 35, Roll 19.

67. Wharton Barker, "The Secret of Russia's Friendship," *Independent*, LVI (March 24, 1904), 647.

5

1. W. E. B. Du Bois, *Black Reconstruction*. New York, 1935, pp. 55–83; Wiley, *Southern Negroes*, pp. 63–84; and Harvey Wish, "Slave Disloyalty under the Confederacy," *Journal of Negro History*, XXIII (October 1938), 435–50.

2. See Fawn M. Brodie, *Thaddeus Stevens, Scourge of the South*. New York, 1959, pp. 158–59.

3. The *Liberator*, January 9, 1863.

4. Phillips, op. cit., vol. I, p. 525.

5. Brodie, op. cit., p. 159.

6. Douglass, op. cit., pp. 389–90.
7. *Atlantic*, XI (February 1863), 240–41.
8. Ibid., XI (March 1863), 288–89.
9. Moncure D. Conway, *Autobiography: Memories and Experiences*. Boston, 1904, vol. I, pp. 378–81.
10. Samuel A. Goddard, *The American Rebellion: Letters on the American Rebellion*. London, 1870, p. 289.
11. Ford, op. cit., p. 243.
12. Quoted in Adams, op. cit., vol. II, p. 112.
13. Lincoln, *Collected Works*, vol. VI, p. 176.
14. Ibid., vol. VI, p. 158.
15. Ibid., vol. VI, pp. 239, 357.
16. Douglass, op. cit., pp. 382–84.
17. Lincoln, *Collected Works*, vol. VI, pp. 408–409.
18. Ibid., vol. VI, p. 291.
19. Ibid., vol. VI, pp. 358, 365, 408, and vol. VII, p. 243.

Index

Welles, Gideon, Secretary of the Navy, 34, 46; and Emancipation Proclamation, suggestions for, 76

Whittier, John Greenleaf (poet), 88; and "The Proclamation" (poem), excerpts from, 118

Wilmot, Senator David, 10

Wilson, Henry, Vice-President of the United States, meeting with Lincoln (Jan. 25, 1863) of, 120

Wright, Elizur (abolitionist), and meeting with Lincoln (Jan. 25, 1863), 119

Wright, Representative Hendrick B., 72

Yeaman, George, 72

"Year of Jubilee" (1863), 92

Zachos, Professor John C., 95

DATE DUE

FEB 2 8 2001		
NOV 0 8 2001		
MAR 1 0 2002		
FEB 0 7 2003		
DEC 1 6 2008		